REVELATION I

REVELATION RECLAIMED

The Use and Misuse of the Apocalypse

Jon Newton

Paternoster:
thinking faith

MILTON KEYNES ● COLORADO SPRINGS ● HYDERABAD

First published 2009 by Paternoster
Paternoster is an imprint of Authentic Media
9 Holdom Avenue, Bletchley, Milton Keynes, Bucks, MK1 1QR, UK
1820 Jet Stream Drive, Colorado Springs, CO 80921, USA
Medchal Road, Jeedimetla Village, Secunderabad 500 055, A.P., India
www.authenticmedia.co.uk

Authentic Media is a division of IBS-STL U.K., limited by guarantee, with its
Registered Office at Kingstown Broadway, Carlisle, Cumbria CA3 0HA.
Registered in England & Wales No. 1216232. Registered charity 270162

British Library Cataloguing in Publication Data

A catalogue record for this book is available from the
British Library

ISBN-13: 978-1-84227-612-9

Cover design by James Kessell for Scratch the Sky Ltd.
(www.scratchthesky.com)
Print Management by Adare
Printed and bound in Great Britain by J. F. Print., Sparkford

Contents

Contents

Chapter 1

STRANGE REVELATIONS

Is Barack Obama the Antichrist? Or maybe Henry Kissinger or Mikhail Gorbachev? Is Bill Gates the 'false prophet' of Revelation 13? Did George Bush, Sr, fire the starter's gun for the race to the end with his call for a 'new world order' after the first Gulf war? Is the world in imminent danger of being devastated by a collision with a large comet? Are recent UN decisions on religion or the environment dangerous conspiracies likely to lay the platform for a world dictatorship? Is the European Community on the road to Antichrist rule? Will we all soon have microchips implanted in our foreheads or hands as part of a new monetary system? Did one of the recent treaties between Israel and the Palestinians (brokered by successive US presidents) start the seven-year countdown to the second coming? Are we about to witness the rebuilding of the Jewish temple (destroyed in AD 70) and the full reinstitution of the Old Testament sacrificial system? Will Russia launch a nuclear attack on Israel? Will a resurgent papacy dominate the planet and enforce Sunday observance on us all?

All this and more has been predicted by Christian writers over the last 40 years. What's more, these predictions have largely been based on two Bible books: Daniel and Revelation.

Some readers take to the latest predictions based on the Bible with great alacrity. Others are put off any investigation of Bible prophecy by the sensational claims made on its behalf. Many more are just puzzled. Surprisingly perhaps, such predictive claims are not new. People have been getting strange revelations out of Revelation for centuries. It's just one of the many barriers to readers of today who want to take Revelation seriously.

Barriers to Reading Revelation

Today's reader isn't going to find Revelation an easy read at the best of times. Its language is weird. Its images are hard to imagine and their meaning even harder to work through. Its worldview is often hard for someone with a modern science-based outlook to accept. Its predictions of 'doom and gloom' are off-putting for those who want to be optimistic about the future. Its warnings of the lake of fire and endless torments with fire and sulphur are at odds with the tolerant Christianity many readers want to embrace.

And some recent commentators on Revelation have attacked it for its disrespectful language about those who disagree with its author, its excessive violence and its attitudes towards women. Some are wondering aloud, what is this book doing in the New Testament? Where is the God of love, forgiveness and grace? For example, the psychiatrist Karl Jung argued that Revelation

> blatantly contradicts all ideas of Christian humility, tolerance, and love of your neighbour and your enemies, and makes nonsense of a loving father in heaven and rescuer of mankind. A veritable orgy of hatred, vindictiveness, and blind destructive fury that revels in fantastic images where terror breaks out and with blood and fire overwhelms a world which Christ had just endeavoured to restore to the original state of innocence and loving communion with God.[1]

But if I had to nominate one particular reason why many readers find Revelation hard to embrace, it would be the way it's been used by preachers and writers in recent years. To begin with, there have been multiple theories explaining what it is about. The proponents of such theories are confident: this is what Revelation means! The trouble is, they contradict each other. And maybe there are even worse problems.

Misuse of the Text

Do you ever have the feeling, when you listen to preaching from Revelation, or read a popular book based on this text, that the preacher/author is somehow misusing it? That they are using the book as a kind of tool for their own agendas or as a kind of propaganda for their favourite causes, or (worse still) as a weapon to attack their enemies with?

Here are a few misuses that seem to appear quite commonly, in my experience:

- *The Nostradamus Syndrome*: predicting what is about to happen, especially in the Middle East or Europe. This reduces Revelation to a kind of secret code. After all, like Nostradamus, it's ambiguous enough to fit a range of scenarios about the future.
- *The Left Behind Threat*: manipulating people to make a decision to follow Christ out of fear that they'll be 'left behind' when Jesus comes and takes away true believers, and have to go through the disasters forecast in Revelation 6–19, the 'great tribulation'.
- *The Conspiracy Theory*: combining bits and pieces of current news with out-of-context verses in Revelation to play on the hearers' or readers' insecurities and increase their fears of a great worldwide conspiracy that usually involves one or more of such seemingly all-powerful groups as the Roman Catholic Church, the United Nations, The European Community, the World Council of Churches, the World Bank, the communists, or others – add al Qaeda or the Taliban to that list now.

Revelation has been twisted to suit so many agendas, interpreted in so many conflicting and incredible ways, that it's no wonder some readers just turn off. As one writer put it,

> [Revelation] . . . has offered all the more opportunity to researchers who can with impunity discover in its pages the message they themselves put there out of a sense that so menacing a document, full of hitherto misunderstood detail, can have application only to the unprecedented world-historical crisis of their own moment in time.[2]

In other words, people read into Revelation whatever they like in order to make it fit their own historical situation!

But it may be said, such attempts to relate Revelation to our day help the cause of evangelism. I am sure they raise awareness of possible interpretations of Revelation and in some cases people do make a commitment to Christ out of fear of coming judgements. But if the evangelists' predictions don't come true, what then? As one evangelical writer commented on Hal Lindsey's *Late Great Planet Earth,*

> It is . . . a very questionable benefit that undermines the credibility of the Church, even if it is true that after reading the book one million people have turned to Christ. The ends still do not justify the means, even if there are a million of them.[3]

In the next few chapters of this book, we will examine such misuses of Revelation more closely. But they raise the question, is there a responsible and fair way to read Revelation? Or is it useless to us today (except maybe as a historical source for early Christianity)?

This is why I decided to write this book. I want to examine ways the book of Revelation has been misused over the centuries, especially in recent days. And I hope to help you, the twenty-first century reader, to make sense of Revelation and profit from reading it. I love the book of Revelation (in spite of the problems noted above), I find it incredibly relevant to my life today, and I hope it won't be thrown into people's intellectual dust bins, but out there doing what its author wanted.

Nothing New Under the Sun

Almost as soon as it was published, the Book of Revelation was subjected to some strange interpretations. Perhaps the earliest one that can be documented was that of the Montanists of the late second century. Montanus, who apparently claimed to be the Holy Spirit incarnate, said that the Last Judgement was at hand and that the New Jerusalem of Revelation 21 would soon descend in Phrygia,[4] near the area to which John originally sent his book.

Even in the early centuries of Christianity the interpretation of Revelation was a 'hot potato'. Chiliasts (who believed in a literal thousand-year reign of Christ on earth) and allegorists (who took the details of Revelation as standing for the Christian's spiritual progress) contended with each other about its true meaning.[5]

Fast forward to the twelfth century and one of the most famous interpreters of Revelation: Joachim of Fiore (in Italy). According to a recent commentary, he was 'arguably the most influential interpreter of the Apocalypse', who 'saw the book as the key to Scripture and the whole of history'.[6] He may be called the father of the so-called 'Historicist' view, which teaches that Revelation contains a fairly detailed prediction of history from the first century to the final end.[7] For example, he believed that the seven heads of the dragon, who tried to devour the child born of the woman (Rev. 12:3), represented six historical figures who had persecuted the church of Christ up to his day, the latest being the Arab leader Saladin (a mighty opponent of the Crusaders), with the seventh still to come.[8] According to Joachim history could be divided into three ages:

> The age of the Father: from creation to the birth of Jesus.
> The age of the Son: beginning with the birth of Jesus.
> The age of the Spirit: beginning after the overthrow of the Antichrist,
> which Joachim expected about 1260.

Apparently, Richard I of England consulted Joachim on his way to attempt to drive Saladin out of Jerusalem and was told that Saladin was the Antichrist and he (Richard) would defeat him. Wrong on both counts![9]

Next, in the thirteenth century, reading Revelation became part of a long struggle between the most powerful leaders of Christian Europe. On one side were the Holy Roman Emperors, Christian rulers of varying amounts of Western Europe.[10] They had the military and political clout. On the other side were the popes, who had the spiritual clout: especially, they could 'excommunicate' rulers they didn't approve of, which in effect 'kicked them out of the church' and technically released their Christian subjects from obeying them.

Two leaders who went into this kind of tussle were Emperor Frederick II and Pope Gregory IX. Frederick was excommunicated twice! Both sides used Revelation in their propaganda war.

Gregory labelled Frederick the beast of Revelation 13:1 and one of Frederick's supporters showed how *Innocencius papa* (one of the pope's titles) had a numerical value of 666 as predicted in Revelation 13:18.[11]

Many of the characters in Revelation have stimulated the imagination of latter day 'prophets' and interpreters. One was the mighty angel of Revelation 10:1–3:

> And I saw another mighty angel coming down from heaven, wrapped in a cloud, with a rainbow over his head; his face was like the sun, and his legs like pillars of fire. He held a little scroll open in his hand. Setting his right foot on the sea and his left foot on the land, he gave a great shout, like a lion roaring.

This angel has been variously identified as

- Jesus;
- the Christian Roman emperors Justin and Justinian;
- Francis of Assisi;
- a leading radical follower of Francis called Peter Olivi; and
- the herald of the Reformation.[12]

Similarly, a famous English 'prophet', Joanna Southcott, claimed in 1814 that she was the woman clothed with the sun predicted in Revelation 12:1, and that she was about to give birth to the messiah. Unfortunately for her followers, she died after her supposed pregnancy, but not before having a great impact on popular culture.[13]

In many such ways, Revelation has been misused by both popular prophets and even scholars. In the next chapter, we examine some specific ways this has happened and is still happening today.

Chapter 2

HOW TO MISUSE REVELATION

The previous chapter has illustrated how Revelation has been misused continually over the centuries. In this chapter, I want to analyze such misuse more closely, so that you can see how it happens, even today, and the seemingly good foundations underneath many current poor interpretations. Let's revisit some of the misuses named in Chapter 1 and a few others besides.

1. The Nostradamus Syndrome: Predicting What Is about to Happen, Especially in the Middle East or Europe

Wait a minute, isn't Revelation all about the future? Doesn't it give us a prediction of future events from our day (or John's day) until the end of history?

Well, yes *and* no. John seems to be mainly predicting events about to occur in his day. He begins by calling his book,

> The revelation of Jesus Christ, which God gave him to show his servants what must *soon* take place (Rev. 1:1).

Then he promises a blessing on those who read, hear and take to heart what is in it,

> because the time is *near* (Rev. 1:3).

Certainly there are future events mentioned in Revelation, such as the second coming of Jesus and the last judgement of all human beings. In that sense, Revelation is a book of predictive prophecy, not only for John's audience but also for us today. Nonetheless, history suggests that using the Book of Revelation to make specific predictions about the future of the world as we now see it leads to confusion, even disaster. It was never intended that we stand with Revelation (or Daniel) in one hand and our newspaper in the other and say, 'That's what's going to happen soon.' It was never meant to be used as some kind of Christian Nostradamus!

How can I be so sure? After all, some of the predictions being made and language used seem to fit so well with current world trends. In fact, one book set out all the predicted events leading up to the second coming in easy-to-follow checklists, starting with events that have already occurred![14] Surely then we can trust that the remaining items will soon follow.

Well, the trouble is, such predictions have been made before and proved totally wrong! More important, they rely on sloppy and inaccurate interpretation of the Bible, including Revelation.

Case 1: A New Political and Economic Order?

New Zealand evangelist Barry Smith for years used Revelation 13 to predict the rise of a world dictator who would cause us all to have some kind of microchip implanted in our heads. After all, Revelation 13:16–17 says,

> He also forced everyone, small and great, rich and poor, free and slave, to receive *a mark on his right hand or on his forehead*, so that no-one could buy or sell unless he had the mark, which is the name of the beast or the number of his name.

He attempted to interpret the number of the beast, 666 (Rev. 13:18), with reference to the seal on the US one-dollar note and the year 1776, the year of the American Declaration of Independence.[15] Somehow the Beast arises out of the New World Order referred to by President George Bush, Sr, the result of a centuries-old conspiracy of Illuminati and Freemasons. But 'Remember this prophecy was predicted in the Book of Revelation 13:16–18 in the year 96 AD and *is being fulfilled between the years 1990 and 2000.*'[16] Unfortunately for Smith and his followers, hindsight shows that he got his dates wrong at least.

Smith wrote a series of books[17] in which he combined current events, conspiracy theories[18] and interpretations of prophecy, particularly Revelation and Daniel, that some readers may find familiar. His basic thesis was as follows:

- The European Union is the 'ten horns' of the beast of Daniel 7:7, 24; Revelation 13:1 and 17:12, the restored Roman Empire.
- From the EU will arise the Antichrist, a secular Jew who will come to power by brokering a peace treaty between Israel and the Arabs,[20] supported by the leader of a one-world church based in Rome (the second beast of Revelation 13).[21]
- Half way through the seven-year peace treaty, he will turn on Israel, stop their sacrifices (which he earlier allowed to be recommenced) and install his statue in Jerusalem,[22] thus introducing the 'great tribulation' of three and a half years.[23]
- His new world order will include a form of ID that will give everyone a number to be invisibly tattooed on their forehead or right hand.[24]

Smith and others speculated that Henry Kissinger, an unbelieving Jew, international statesman and former US Secretary of State, could be the man, or at least was preparing the way for him.[25] This idea may have begun with George Otis, whose book *The Ghost of Hagar* appeared the year after the Yom Kippur (Arab-Israeli) War of 1973 and arose from Kissinger's role as peace-maker in that conflict.

Similarly, Jeff Beacham writes,

> I believe that Bible prophesy [sic] asserts that there will be an interconnection between a false religious system and the economic and political powers within the European Community. The combination of this will be revealed, of course, when an individual called in prophesy the "false prophet" assists the Antichrist (who will rise to rule the new Europe) in implementing the ultimate economic system where human beings are reduced to individual economic units through a "mark" on their right hand or forehead (see Revelation 13:16–18).[27]

This comment seems quite relevant in these days of economic rationalism and globalization, but the link between a religious and an economic system is lacking, in spite of Beacham's claim that the mark is a kind of microchip implant.[28] This might be technically feasible, but Revelation tells us it is imposed by the religious side of the conspiracy as part of a campaign of enforced worship (Rev. 13:11–17).

Consider these extracts from Revelation 13:

- They *worshipped* the beast (v. 4)
- All the inhabitants of the earth will *worship* the beast (v. 8)
- Then I saw another beast, coming out of the earth. He had two horns like a lamb, but he spoke like a dragon. He . . . made the earth and its inhabitants *worship* the first beast . . . he performed great and miraculous signs . . . He ordered them to set up an image in honour of the beast who was wounded by the sword and yet lived. He was given power to give breath to the image of the first beast, so that it could speak and cause all who refused to *worship* the image to be killed (vv. 11–15).

Until the second beast arises, and people are worshipping the first beast, microchips cannot be prophetically significant.

Case 2: A New Temple?

Other attempts to predict the course of the future from Revelation have been equally frustrating, even when apparently promising. Thus commentators of the Historicist school during the late nineteenth century, with their Bibles in one hand and contemporary evidence in the other, *were* able to successfully forecast the downfall of the Ottoman Turkish Empire and the return of the Jews to Palestine.[29] When the British declared their intention to facilitate a Jewish homeland in the famous Balfour Declaration (1917), such predictions seemed vindicated.[30] However, the same writers also predicted the decline of Islam, which looked feasible then, but was certainly premature.

Perhaps the most common prediction made by many Futurist[31] interpreters of Revelation, Daniel and other prophetic passages in the Bible is that the Jewish temple will be rebuilt and the Old Testament sacrificial system restored.[32] The original temple, constructed under Solomon shortly after 1000 BC, was destroyed by the Chaldeans (Babylonians) in 587 BC. The second temple in Jerusalem, originally built in Ezra's time (around 516 BC), was dramatically reconstructed by Herod the Great and his successors around the time of Jesus, reaching completion in AD 62. But it was destroyed by the Roman armies who besieged Jerusalem during the Roman-Jewish war of AD 66–70 and has never been rebuilt. A Muslim mosque occupies part of the site, but the 'wailing wall' remains as part of the ruins.

Will the temple be rebuilt? Rumours abound of Jewish groups planning to undertake this task, sometimes with funding from Christians in the US. In one case four Jewish youths were caught plotting the destruction of the Muslim holy places on the temple mount.[33] Interestingly, there was an attempt to rebuild the temple as long ago as 368 under the anti-Christian Roman emperor Julian.

> The Roman historian Amianus Marcellinus had reported that those efforts were frustrated by the appearance of mysterious balls of fire which prevented the workmen from building. Julian was warned by Christians that the Temple could not be rebuilt until the Antichrist appeared.[34]

Most of the scriptural warrant for such an expectation lies outside Revelation, which never predicts any such event.[35] However, it allows the interpreters concerned to see the events described in Revelation 11, where John is ordered to 'measure the temple of God and the altar' (v. 1), as happening in modern-day Jerusalem with a literal temple.[36]

This kind of interpretation, however, has the effect of cutting-off Revelation from its New Testament roots. Revelation never speaks of revived sacrifices and such a development would be extremely surprising in the light of the theology of atonement found in Hebrews 9–10, where the old covenant system of sacrifices is described as obsolete and the truly legitimate temple is that in heaven, which Revelation affirms. Consider, for example, Revelation 8:3–5; 11:19 ('God's temple in heaven was opened') and 15:5 ('in heaven the temple, that is, the tabernacle of the Testimony, was opened'). Like the author of Hebrews, Revelation presents the atoning death of Jesus as central to history (Rev. 5;

12:11) and in his vision of the future there is no temple in the New Jerusalem (Rev. 21:22). Hence the temple mentioned in Revelation 11:1 is more likely a reference to conditions prior to AD 70 (when the Jerusalem temple was destroyed by the Romans) or else refers to the church as the temple of the Spirit (as in 1 Cor. 3:16, 17).

Certain writers called 'dispensationalists' (because they see history as divided by God into seven eras or dispensations) also uniformly predict a future period of intense suffering for the Jews. Since, in their view, the true church of Christ is 'raptured' to heaven before the tribulation and the rule of the Antichrist, the troubles described in Revelation 6–19 (the tribulation) are experienced by the unbelieving world, and especially the Jews, though in their case it will cause many of them (the 144,000 mentioned in Rev. 7:4–8; 14:1–5) to convert to Christ and become flaming Jewish evangelists and martyrs.[37]

I am not a prophet and I can't guarantee that the Jewish temple won't ever be reconstructed. However, such speculation seems to me to divert attention from the true message of Revelation and the primary commission for Christians, which is not to try to fulfil prophecy (such as by getting lots of Jews into Israel to be slaughtered by the Antichrist or by raising funds for temple reconstruction), but to win the whole world to Christ. This seems to be what Jesus was emphasizing in Acts 1:6–8. In answer to the question from his disciples, 'will you at this time restore the kingdom to Israel?', Jesus warns them that 'it is not for you to know'; instead they will be filled with the power of the Holy Spirit so as to bear witness to Jesus all over the world.

Case 3: New Sunday Laws?

A current website boldly predicts, 'A new world order is about to start: are you ready for it?'[38] It goes on to identify the beast from the sea in Revelation 13 as the Roman Catholic Church, the second beast as the United States, and the mark of the beast as observance of a Sunday Sabbath day: 'Soon, through universal Sunday laws, Satan will make it a crime to obey God.' So should we be looking for a universal ID system, a rebuilt temple or universal Sunday laws?

This highlights another problem with this approach to reading Revelation: different groups are looking for different events and we can always find something that might turn out the way we expect. For instance, Seventh-day Adventist interpreters, like those behind this website,[39] are always looking for news of Sunday observance being made compulsory somewhere, because that is what their view of Revelation and other prophecies leads them to expect as the mark of the beast.

Other Cases

Both Historicist and Futurist commentators of the 1970s and 1980s, when communism and the USSR seemed such a threat, often predicted a Russian attack on Israel (out of prophecies in *Ezekiel*),[40] a Russian take-over of Western Europe leading to the destruction of both the European Community and the papacy,[41] or a Russian war with the USA. For example, a retired US general in about 1950 wrote that the US was probably referred to in Revelation 8:8, which says that 'a huge mountain, all ablaze, was thrown into the sea' so that 'A third of the sea turned into blood.' This he saw as referring to a surprise atomic attack by Russia that would destroy America.[42] Since the fall of the USSR and its 'empire', this now looks less likely, if not impossible.

Various passages from Revelation have been used as the basis for predictions over the years, only to have to be reinterpreted when the predicted events don't happen. For example, the drying up of the Euphrates 'to prepare the way for the kings from the east' (Rev. 16:12) seems to be one of the most specific 'predictions' in the book. A Puritan writer of 1621 used this to predict that the river would literally dry up to allow the Jews to return to Palestine.[43] A nineteenth-century preacher, John Cumming, saw the dried up river as signifying the fall of Islam, allowing the Jews to migrate from all nations, including China.[44] Recently, however, Australian preacher Jeff Beacham pointed out that the building of Turkey's Ataturk Dam now makes it possible for the Euphrates River to be literally dried up and comments on the growing power of Asia that would make an Eastern invasion with 200 million soldiers a real possibility (Rev. 16:12; 9:14–16).[45]

Some of the current predictions may come true, but many will prove false. Using Revelation to predict the near future of our day is a risky, if exciting, strategy. But ultimately it undermines the credibility of the interpreters and the book itself.

2. The News Commentary Approach: Finding Fulfilments of Prophecy in Current Events and Trends

'It is becoming more difficult for cynics, both in and out of the church, to deny the fact that almost daily, major world events are fulfilling prophecies spoken of in the Bible over many thousands of years,' writes Jeff Beacham.[46] And Tim LaHaye agrees, 'Only a biblical illiterate is unable to see that these are the last days.'[47] As well as using Revelation to make predictions, some writers also use it to interpret trends in current events – this is sometimes facetiously called 'newspaper exegesis' since it uses news reports to interpret Revelation. Now I believe Revelation does give us a new perspective on world history and reality. But does it really offer a running commentary on current trends 2000 years after it was written?

Various trends of the twentieth century particularly have helped make dodgy interpretations of Revelation more credible. Apart from the establishment of modern Israel, there have been the development of nuclear weapons, computers and credit cards and the growth of European unity and Chinese power.[48] For example, many writers have speculated on the economic sanctions implied by Revelation 13:16–18, which says that people would not be able to buy or sell without the mark of the beast. Bringing together developments in technology and the world economy, it is not hard to see plastic money leading to identity marks on people's bodies in a new cashless world.[49] Hence when Australia's leading banks introduced a common credit card called 'Bankcard' in the 1970s, many serious Bible students noted that its design of three stylized 'b's looked suspiciously like '666'.[50] A sign of a worldwide financial conspiracy perhaps?

What about the current emphasis on global warming and ecological crisis? After all, some of the events apparently predicted by John are ecological disasters: scorching heat (Rev. 16:8, 9; global warming or the depletion of the ozone layer perhaps?), bitter waters (Rev. 8:10, 11) and destruction of vegetation (Rev. 8:7). Maybe Revelation is warning us against the dangers of pollution and misuse of the world's resources.[51]

Or perhaps Revelation is foretelling a conspiracy of Greens and New Agers. For instance, the late Barry Smith linked Green wilderness groups with Revelation 17:3 because there 'the angel carried me away in the Spirit into a desert (or wilderness)', where 'I saw a woman sitting on a scarlet beast that was covered with blasphemous names and had seven heads and ten horns.' Here is Smith's conclusion:

> From the above information, we can see that the spiritual habitat of the end time world may be referred to as a 'wilderness'. *Strangely enough, the hierarchy of the Illuminati and all of their subordinate witches and occultists also refer to their new age of Aquarius as a wilderness.* This is a spiritual place within the embrace of Mother Earth where all people can be absorbed in collective thought and blend as one people without individuality in a blissful state of the lostness of the mind.[52]

Whatever the truth of Smith's attack on Green politics or New Agers, it beggars belief to infer that this is what Revelation is referring to! At the very least, Smith's 'interpretation' depends on some very shaky assumptions about the intended audience of John's text.

Moreover, many previous readers have seen their struggles as interpreted by passages in Revelation. For instance, the radical Franciscans[53] of the thirteenth century, caught up in a struggle to preserve the rule of poverty taught by Francis of Assisi, sometimes saw Francis as inaugurating a time of renewal indicated by the sixth and seventh seals of Revelation and viewed the Babylon prostitute (Rev. 17) and the synagogue of Satan (Rev. 2:9; 3:9) as standing for worldliness in the church.[54]

In the sixteenth and seventeenth centuries, England was wracked by struggles over religion. Many English writers therefore saw Revelation fulfilled in the momentous events of their day, dominated by the threat of the papacy and its conspiring with nations like Spain to invade England. For instance, Thomas

Simmons saw the accession of the mildly Protestant Queen Elizabeth I (1558), after the martyrdoms under Catholic Queen Mary,[55] as fulfilling the cry of the martyrs in Revelation 6:9–11;[56] Edmund Spenser even saw Elizabeth as the woman 'clothed with the sun' in Revelation 12:1.[57] Another writer saw the defeat of the Spanish Armada (which attempted to invade England on behalf of Roman Catholicism) as predicted by Revelation 15:2, which describes a sea of glass mixed with fire.[58] Others found prophetic significance in the execution of King Charles I (1649)[59] and in the events of 1688, the 'Glorious Revolution' which sent Catholic King James II into exile and thus saved Britain from the return of Roman Catholicism.[60]

With even more reason, the events flowing from the French Revolution seemed to many to be a fulfilment of prophecy, with the downfall of the great Roman conspiracy, papal political power. As Ernest Sandeen describes it,

> As the unbelievable events of the 1790s unfolded, students of . . . apocalyptic literature became convinced (in a rare display of unanimity) that they were witnessing the fulfillment of the prophecies of Daniel 7 and Revelation 13 . . . the final act occurred in 1798 when French troops under Berthier marched on Rome, established a republic, and sent the pope into banishment. Commentators were quick to point out that this 'deadly wound' received by the papacy *had been explicitly described and dated in Revelation 13.* Although prophetic scholars had previously been unable to agree on what dates to assign to the rise and fall of papal power, it now became clear, after the fact, that the papacy had come to power in 538 AD [i.e. 1260 years before 1798; see Rev. 11:3; 12:6].[61]

Seventh-day Adventists still build their interpretation of history on the basis of identifying certain verses in Revelation with specific events in European and American history. For instance, the 'great earthquake' of Revelation 6:12 becomes the Lisbon earthquake of 1755; the sun turning black and the moon blood-red is seen as fulfilled by events in north-eastern America in May 19–20, 1780; and the stars falling to earth happened in a great meteorite shower of November 13, 1833.[62] These events have become part of the story of the birth of the Adventist church.[63]

In a similar way, Jehovah's Witnesses saw the suppression and incarceration of Witnesses by the Nazis, abetted by the Roman Catholic Church, as related to the blood guilt of Babylon: 'In her was found the blood of prophets and of the saints, and of all who have been killed on the earth' (Rev. 18:24).[64] They also continue to proclaim the prophetic significance of 1914 as initiating the end times and their mission to the whole earth:

> Bible prophecy shows that God's Kingdom under Christ was set up in 1914 and is now poised to crush Satan's entire system. That Kingdom is ready to 'go subduing in the midst of [Christ's] enemies.'[65]

More recently the threat of nuclear war has influenced many people's thinking about Revelation. Many of the worldwide catastrophes described in the text seem to be more credible if interpreted as a nuclear holocaust; such as Revelation 8:6–12 (the term 'wormwood' has even been related to the Chernobyl disaster)[66] and the Armageddon scenes of Revelation 16:14, 16 and 19:19–21.[67] Hal Lindsey has been a leader in this trend, effortlessly translating Revelation's imagery into descriptions of modern warfare; for example, the 'hail and fire mixed with blood . . . hurled down upon the earth' (Rev. 8:7) represent nuclear missiles and the details of the seven bowls in Revelation 16 describe the effects of nuclear bombs, such as the radiation (Rev. 16:2, 9).[68]

In a similar way, some Futurist interpreters of Revelation identify developments in economics, technology or other world affairs that make a 'literal' reading of some passages more credible than in earlier days. For example, Tim LaHaye speculates that 'ours is the first generation that can literally see the fulfilment of 11:9' (the public display of the bodies of the two witnesses) by the medium of satellite television.[69] It's tempting – it seemingly makes Revelation so relevant – but it's also very dangerous. This kind of running prophetic commentary can also quickly become out of date when world trends shift.

3. The Favoured Son Claim: Finding a Special Place for a Particular Sect or Nation

Another related misuse of Revelation is to use it to identify 'our' group as somehow special in the plan of God, maybe the only ones who will make it to heaven, or at least specially honoured in God's new world. Thus we are the church of Philadelphia (Rev. 3:7–13), the 144,000 sealed with God's seal (Rev. 7:3, 4), the overcoming Christians (Rev. 2:7; 12:11), the saints opposed by the beast (Rev. 13:10), the inhabitants of the new heavens and/or earth (Rev. 21) or at least those whose names are in the Lamb's book (Rev. 13:8; 20:15).

The most famous example of this is the Jehovah's Witnesses' use of the two passages related to the number 144,000 (Rev. 7:4–8; 14:1–5). For them, this group is the core of their number, the most favoured of their heroes. They also claim to be the great multitude described in Revelation 7:9, drawn from 'every nation, tribe, people and language', as this statement from the official website indicates:

> Millions of Jehovah's Witnesses sincerely try to live in harmony with God's instructions and ways. Their hope of eternal life is anchored in God's new world. By conducting their daily lives in obedience to God's laws, they show him their willingness to submit to his way of ruling both now and in the new world. Everywhere, regardless of their nationality or race, they obey the same standards—those set out by God in his Word. That is why they are a true international brotherhood, a new world society of God's making.[70]

Seventh-day Adventists attempted to envisage themselves as the persecuted saints or remnant in Revelation, being opposed by the papal Beast (Rev. 13) because they refuse to move their Sabbath observance to a Sunday, which is the mark of the beast (Rev. 13:16–18).[71] At least they understood the *religious* significance of the events of Revelation 13.

Some medieval writers identified the seal of God placed on the foreheads of His followers (Rev. 7:3; 9:4) with the stigmata of Francis of Assisi[72] and saw the Franciscans as having a special place in Revelation.[73] Francis was even identified with Elijah as one of the witnesses of Revelation 11:3 who 'prophesy for 1,260 days, clothed in sackcloth'.[74]

Now it is arguable that John is also heroizing his followers, but in his case the heroes are Christians in general, at least those who 'overcome' and do Jesus' will to the end (Rev. 2:26), who are willing to suffer and die for their faith (Rev. 12:11). Hence, Christians suffering persecution have always found great encouragement from Revelation, not necessarily because they are a select favoured group but because they are challenged by the text to endure faithfully. The danger of identifying one *particular* church or Christian group with the images of Revelation is that this makes other Christians 'outsiders', even enemies.

Another form of the same mistake is to identify *specific nations or ethnic groups* in terms of God's destiny and match them with symbols or descriptions in Revelation. The most famous attempt to do this has been made by 'British Israelites', who believe that the Anglo-Saxon peoples (represented by the British and Nordic nations, the USA and/or British Common-wealth of Nations) are the true descendants of the 'lost' tribes of Israel. Hence the 144,000 of Revelation 7 and 14, or the woman clothed with the sun, of Revelation 12, are easily identified with these nations or peoples.[75] In this way, Anglo-Celts could logically claim, 'God is on our side' or 'God has a special destiny for us.'

Similar claims were made about the USA in its earlier days of Puritan revivalism, when it seemed that the new nation must have a special place in God's program.[76] In fact, Christopher Columbus himself saw his discovery of the new world as a fulfilment of Revelation 21, with its talk of a 'new earth'.[77]

More frequently, dispensationalist commentators see in their Bibles (not just Revelation) a central future role for the Jews and the state of Israel, one which leads them to see Israel's rebirth as a nation (1948) and subsequent re-occupation of Jerusalem (1967) as striking fulfilments of biblical prophecy. They frequently go on to agitate for Christians to support Israel politically.[78] Based more on passages such as Luke 21:24 (where Jesus predicts that 'Jerusalem will be trampled underfoot by the Gentiles *until* the times of the Gentiles are fulfilled') and Ezekiel 37–39 (which speaks of a reborn Israel and a coming invasion from the north), such commentators see these twentieth-century developments as signs of the impending end and the second coming.[79] They then read these expectations into Revelation when they interpret the 144,000 (Rev. 7:4–8) or the coming battle of Armageddon (Rev. 16:12–16). For them Israel (or the Jews) must be the central nation and we as Christians must support her. This has significant political implications in today's world, especially in US politics.

4. The Conspiracy Theory: Enemy-Bashing and Fear-Mongering

If some interpreters want to use Revelation to paint themselves as the 'in group' of the church, there are others who want to use the text to demonize their enemies and stoke fear of conspiracies. For example, Tim LaHaye uses his commentary on Revelation to attack secular humanism in education,[80] the ecumenical movement[81] and the Roman Catholic Church.[82] All of these are portrayed as enemies of the true faith or true church, conspiring to attack it and establish the rule of the Antichrist.

A number of recent interpreters of Revelation claim that John himself is writing to oppose and demonize *his* enemies within the churches of Asia, calling them unflattering names from the Old Testament like 'Balaam' and 'Jezebel' (Rev. 2:14, 20). Certainly John paints a very negative picture of what appears to be the Roman Empire, and the imperial cult especially,[83] and this imagery has proved capable of being applied to enemies of the church in successive generations, whether it be the Inquisition on the one hand, or Muslims, Communists, Nazis, liberals and others on the other. Moreover, John's view of humanity is starkly dualistic: there are those whose names are on the Lamb's book of life and there are those who follow the beast (Rev. 13:8). But before we identify our group as the former, or our opponents as the latter, let's pause to consider previous attempts to do this.

The Prostitute Model

The prostitute Babylon (Rev. 17) has been a particularly tempting image to identify with enemies of various believers, beginning obviously with the Roman Empire itself. Protestants for years saw it as a portrayal of the Roman Catholic Church, which would eventually be destroyed by its political allies.[84] In some cases, the pope was also the beast of Revelation 13.[85] Even so brilliant a man as Sir Isaac Newton spent many hours researching and writing in this vein.[86] The decline of papal political power in the nineteenth century seemed to vindicate them on one level, but this failed to lead on to other events of prophecy, thus calling their interpretation into question.

A more recent attempt to connect the prostitute with the Roman Catholic Church comes from the pen of Dave Hunt, though he combines this interpretation of Revelation 17 with a Futurist view of Revelation, which enables him to see the Roman Catholic Church as the core of a *future* world religion. Most of Hunt's *argument* is based, however, on the *past* errors and crimes attributable to the papacy.[87]

But this is not the only possibility. For instance, a seventeenth-century Baptist called Anne Wentworth, whose abusive husband had ejected her from her home, saw the whore as a portrayal of patriarchal society.[88] Some ancient and modern commentators have seen the whore as unbelieving Jews or first-century Jerusalem.[89] Others saw references to Muslims or Turks.[90] Pro-American writers of the eighteenth and nineteenth centuries sometimes saw the prostitute as a European monarchist confederacy opposed to the new world Christian republic,[91] a view reflected in more recent ruminations about the current European Community.

More recently, she has been seen as foreshadowing a great worldwide religious confederacy, perhaps beginning with the World Council of Churches[92] or New Age spirituality.[93] For example, John F. Walvoord confidently states,

> For centuries, expositors have recognized the harlot as the symbol of religion and the scarlet beast as representing the political power of the Mediterranean Confederacy in the end time. While their alliance will bring a temporary stability to the world, it will also create a blasphemous religious system which will lead the world to new depths of immorality and departure from true faith in God.[94]

Walvoord sees the ecumenical movement and occult influence in the mainline churches as foreshadowing this development of a 'super church' in alliance with the Antichrist; thus this interpretation of prophecy allows him to attack such bodies as the World Council of Churches.[95]

However, in the times of Saddam Hussein and the two Gulf wars, a new possibility emerged: perhaps Babylon (Rev. 17–19) was meant literally and this ancient city was about to be revived, as Saddam was attempting to achieve.[96] Tim LaHaye, for example, writes, 'I am inclined to believe that the weight of biblical prophecy requires the literal rebuilding of Babylon',[97] as happens in the novel *Left Behind*.

The Beast Model

The beast(s) of Revelation 13 have always been a fruitful mine for enemy bashing and conspiracy theories. Many Protestant Historicists saw the beast's 42-month or 1260-day dominance as fulfilled by the rise of papal power in 538 and its crushing under Napoleon in 1798; Seventh-day Adventists still hold a similar view.[98] But other possible villains have included:

- Roman emperors Nero or Domitian or the Roman Empire generally.
- Leaders of the Jewish revolt against Rome in 66.
- Various medieval emperors.
- Archbishop Laud in seventeenth-century Britain.[99]
- George III of Britain.[100]
- Hitler.[101]
- Mussolini.[102]
- The United States (as enforcers of Sunday).
- The 'Anglo-American World Power'.[103]
- A leader emerging from the European Community.[104]

In fact, as long ago as the third century, the Christian theologian Hippolytus suggested that the Antichrist would rule over a ten-nation successor to, or revival of, the Roman Empire, based on Daniel 2 (the ten toes of the statue), Daniel 7 (the ten horns of the fourth beast), Revelation 13 (the first beast also has ten crowned horns) and Revelation 17 (ten horns equated with ten kings who will rule with the beast). It is only a short jump from here to seeing the post-war trend towards European unity as prophetically significant.[105]

Other Enemies: Muslims, Asians, Arabs, even Christians!

The rise of Islam, and later the Ottoman empire, was frequently read into Revelation by Christian interpreters from medieval times, since this was a frightening threat to them. The fifth trumpet, followed by a star falling from heaven and its consequential locust plague, was often seen as symbolizing the fall of Muhammad and the spread of Islam,[106] if it didn't stand for false ministers, especially Catholics.[107] Some interpreters saw Gog and Magog as standing for Muslims or Turks.[108]

Other interpreters saw various heresies or Christian figures they disliked reflected in Revelation's imagery. For example, Luther identified the falling star (Wormwood) of Revelation 8:10–11 with the third-century theologian Origen, whereas another Protestant writer saw it as the fourth-century heretic Nestorius. Others took it to mean Thomas Aquinas or Luther.[109]

At times, this trend has meant that writers on Revelation even descend into racism, especially when writing about 'the kings from the East' (Rev. 16:12) and the 200-million strong army associated with the eastern boundaries of Israel or the Roman world (Rev. 9:14–16). The numbers alone evoke traditional western fears of yellow hordes and a chapter in Hal Lindsey's *Late Great Planet Earth* is actually entitled 'The Yellow Peril'.[110] While rhetorically appealing to western readers, this approach undermines or ignores the affirmation of Revelation that every nation is represented in the innumerable host of the Lamb (Rev. 5:9; 7:9). Thus in the minds of these authors, the dangers associated with the rising power of China, for example, overshadow the amazing rise in the numbers of Chinese Christians, which is more accurately a fulfilment of Revelation!

The Arabs have also become enemies in the minds of many evangelical and fundamentalist Christians. This is the 'flipside' of the unwavering support of Israel that has come out of dispensational premillennialism. While the Scriptures used for this are derived largely from the Old Testament (such as the passages about Ishmael, especially Gen. 16:10–12), the hostility towards the Arabs has tended to be based largely on their adherence to Islam (Arab Christians are forgotten) and their resistance to the state of Israel, which led to the dispossession of Palestinians who had lived there for centuries. But this hostility is then imported into scenarios based on Revelation; for example, the Arabs are seen as part of an invading army led by Russia or China against Israel.

So maybe this 'enemy bashing' out of Revelation has to be seen for what it is: an unsubtle misuse of the text.

5. The Separation Line: Justifying a New Religious or Political Movement

Revelation calls on true Christians to be separated from 'Babylon':

> Come out of her, my people,
> So that you will not share in her sins,
> So that you will not receive any of her plagues (Rev. 18:4).

Several Christian movements have justified their existence and separation from the church of their day on the basis of this call. For example, the Seventh-day Adventists used these themes to argue for separation from a compromised Protestantism still partial to Sunday observance, which was supposedly instituted by the papacy.

Kovacs and Rowland describe a different case in seventeenth-century Bristol (England):

> Dorothy Hazzard was one of the 'professors of the city' who 'began to lead the way out of Babylon' and decided to separate themselves from 'hearing Common Prayer'... Her growing conviction that the Baptist and Anabaptist reformation had much to commend it meant separating from her [Anglican clergyman] husband's pattern of worship and attracting the opprobrium of contemporaries . . . the Apocalypse emboldened her to take the decisive step . . .[113]

Similarly, early Pentecostals saw themselves as a group with a unique place in heralding the last days and often called on believers to 'come out' of religious Babylon, meaning the more traditional churches.

But not all such attempts have been so harmless. Remember the 'Branch Davidians' of Waco, Texas? This little cult, originally a breakaway from the Seventh-day Adventist Church, was taken over by one Vernon Howell. He then changed his name to David Koresh to indicate his claim to be the 'anointed one', like the Persian emperor Cyrus (see Isaiah 45:1).[112] He also claimed to be the Lamb who would open the seals (Rev. 5) and the conqueror on the white horse of Revelation 6:2. The 'marriage supper of the Lamb' (Rev. 19:9) was interpreted to support his begetting children through wives of his followers.

When US federal agents raided the property to investigate polygamy and child abuse reports, some of the group resisted, encouraged by Revelation 6:9–11, which 'predicted' that some would be killed.[113] Koresh also saw himself as the seventh angel of Revelation 10:7 and saw his work as the last of the seven thunders in Revelation 10.[114] He believed, from Revelation 8:5, that 'his last act on earth would be to start an eschatological fire'.[115] Instead it was his sect which experienced a fiery and violent end when the federal agents finally attacked their compound in 1993. Yet as late as 1996, the remaining Branch Davidians 'expected David Koresh to return as the rider on the white horse, to lead his followers in the mass slaughter of the wicked'.[116]

Conclusion

Obviously then, Revelation has been horribly misused over the centuries. Some of the most common cases in recent years have come out of a system of interpreting the Bible known as dispensationalism. It's a big word, but chances are you have encountered this system in a Christian novel, movie or popular prophecy book, such as the *Left Behind* series.

Chapter 3

THE LEFT BEHIND THREAT

If you're interested in Revelation, or in the 'end times' of history, you've probably read books in the *Left Behind* series or seen the movies, or at least heard about them. This series of novels imaginatively creates a scenario for the last seven years of this age based on dispensational premillennialism. Let's unpack this term:

Dispensationalism teaches that God has administered his plan for history over seven periods called 'dispensations'. Each of them ends in human failure and a direct intervention by God. Passages in the Bible are assigned strictly to just one of the dispensations. The word 'church' describes the international company of believers in this age only: after the rapture, the church goes to heaven forever (see 1 Thess. 4:17) and the Jews resume centre stage. This is known as *pretribulationism* ('pretrib' for short), because the rapture of believers comes before the great end time tribulation.

Premillennialists believe that Jesus' second coming precedes the establishment of a literal kingdom on earth ruled by Jesus and His followers and lasting for exactly 1,000 years (based on Rev. 20). Not all premillennialists are dispensationalists or pretributionists, however, as we will see. Some believe that the church will experience all or part of the coming tribulation.

LaHaye has his own version of dispensationalism. The *Left Behind* novels begin with the 'rapture', which most dispensationalists see as an instant mass disappearance of true believers all over the world, and lead the reader through the events of the 'great tribulation' (Rev. 7:14) as experienced by the fictional heroes of the novels. The first event referred to is an invasion of Israel by Russia, which comes unstuck when Russia's missiles and jets are miraculously destroyed, leaving not a single Israeli casualty. Then in the rapture itself, the sudden disappearance of millions causes confusion, and havoc in places where those taken were drivers or pilots. All abortion clinics are temporarily out of business with the disappearance of all infants and unborn babies.[117] The first book contains an imaginative reconstruction of a flight during which a number of passengers and crew disappear, leaving their clothes behind (a somewhat humorous touch).

As the unbelieving world tries to make sense of these disappearances, and adjust to the effects, a new world ruler is manoeuvred into power by wealthy bankers. He initiates a peace treaty with Israel and eliminates everyone who gets in the way, including some of his sponsors. Simultaneously a new world religion is being created to support his rule (supposedly based on the two beast figures of Rev. 13, the beast proper and the false prophet, as he is called in Rev. 19:20).

Well-written novels and dramatic movies often have the effect of causing the reader to imaginatively enter the fictional world created by the author, suspending critical thinking. In this case, the authors' use of language derived from Revelation, Daniel and other prophetic books creates the sense that they are interpreting the Bible accurately. This may be one reason why the genre of prophecy novels has flourished since the 1930s.[118] However, leaving aside the question of the credibility of the scenarios described in these novels, some questions need to be raised about their interpretation of Revelation.

1. Can the Idea of a Sudden Disappearance of Faithful Christians Be Found in Revelation?

This idea is derived from several Bible passages:

- 1 Thessalonians 4:17, where the resurrection of dead saints is followed by the living believers being 'caught up . . . to meet the Lord in the air';

- Luke 17:34–35, where out of two people, one is 'taken' and the other 'left';
- 1 Corinthians 15:51–52, where Paul speaks of the dead being raised imperishable and others being changed at the last trumpet; and
- 2 Thessalonians 2:6–8, which states that the 'man of lawlessness' is held back from being revealed until the one holding him back 'is taken out of the way'.

In none of these passages are the saints said to 'disappear'; this is read into the text by dispensationalists. Their case is much weaker, however, when we turn to Revelation.

Certain passages in Revelation are appealed to for support of this teaching. In Revelation 3:10, the church at Philadelphia is promised, 'I will also keep you from the hour of trial that is going to come upon the whole world to test those who live on the earth.' LaHaye takes this to mean that they are 'raptured' out of harm's way, but the verse does not actually say that and it is addressed to only one of the seven churches. In order to make this interpretation work, LaHaye must argue that this church is not really the literal first-century church in Philadelphia,[119] but stands for an era of the church that will exist when Jesus comes, even though it is the *second to last* church addressed, not the last.[120] It is far more likely to be a specific promise of protection during the Roman persecutions of early Christians; elsewhere LaHaye admits God can protect people in the midst of the tribulation.[121]

The voice calling John to 'come up here' to be shown 'what must take place after this' (Rev. 4:1) is taken as a kind of model of the rapture, especially in the light of Revelation's failure to mention the word 'church' after this. Some such interpretation is essential to the pretribulation view, in which the true church is absent from earth during the seven-year tribulation supposedly described in Revelation 6–19. But this interpretation has serious problems. This verse describes not a bodily 'rapture' but a specific revelatory experience 'in the Spirit' given to just one person over 1,900 years ago. Thus even LaHaye admits that 'the Rapture of the Church is not explicitly taught in Revelation 4'.[122]

But what about the absence of the word 'church' in Revelation 4–19? Does this imply that all true believers in Jesus are gone? Who then are the martyrs still coming to join those 'under the altar' in Revelation 6:9–11? Who are the 144,000 sealed 'servants of God' (Rev. 7:3), later described as redeemed followers of the Lamb (Rev. 14:1–5)? Who are the saints whose prayers go up to God and help forward His plans (Rev. 8:3, 4)? What about the two witnesses of Revelation 11: do they not qualify to be part of the church in view of their faithful witness, martyrdom and resurrection? Who are the conquerors whose faith in Jesus' blood and faithful testimony defeat the accusations of the devil and cause him to be thrown down (Rev. 12:10, 11)? Who are the children of the woman who keep God's commandments and the testimony of Jesus (Rev. 12:17)? Who are the 'saints' who are oppressed by the beast (Rev. 13:7) and are called on to endurance and faith (Rev. 13:10): apparently their names are written in the Lamb's book of Life (Rev. 13:8), like all the other believers!

Who are the saints mentioned in Revelation 14:12, who are urged to endure and hold fast their faith in Jesus? And who are those who will die in the Lord 'from now on' (Rev. 14:13)? And who are those who conquer the beast, its image and the number of its name (Rev. 15:2)? Who is Revelation 16:15 addressed to, with its warning to stay awake and clothed in view of Jesus' coming, right in the middle of preparations for the battle of Armageddon? Who are the saints, prophets and witnesses to Jesus killed by the whore (Rev. 17:6; 18:24; 19:2)? Who are the 'called and chosen and faithful' who accompany the Lamb in defeating the ten kings (Rev. 17:14)? And who are the ones called God's people who are urged to come out of Babylon (Rev. 18:4)?

Clearly the language used to describe these people sounds very like the language used of Christians elsewhere in the New Testament. Hence pretribulationist authors have to invent a bunch of 'tribulation saints' who are somehow Christians but not part of the church, contradicting the rest of the New Testament. Dispensationalists get very subtle here with their fine definitions of 'church'; at least they have their work cut out for them getting around the texts just mentioned. For example, LaHaye makes the astounding claim that 'not one verse can be found in the New Testament instructing Christians on how to live during that seven-year period'[123] (the tribulation). Yet he spends his book, and the *Left Behind* novels, showing how Revelation does just that!

But what about Revelation 7:9–17? Does not this describe the church, made up of people of all nations, now safely removed from the great tribulation and standing before God in heaven? But they are said to have come *out of* the great tribulation (Rev. 7:14), not removed before that event begins. In fact, LaHaye predicts an exciting and unprecedented worldwide harvest of souls during the tribulation, 'the greatest revival the world has ever known',[124] based in this chapter. It sounds so exciting it almost tempts the reader to want to be 'left behind' in order to be part of it.[125] And yet they are somehow not the church, even though they act like it! Similarly the congregation that gathers in the novel *Left Behind* seems like quite a good church, but must be 'a special company'.[126]

Mid-tribulationists (who expect the true church to be raptured midway through the tribulation) appeal to the snatching up of the male child (Rev. 12:5), followed by the persecution of the child's mother and 'the rest of her offspring' (Rev. 12:6, 13–17). This is a lot more plausible, especially since these events lead into the beast episodes in chapters 13–14, but there are still Christians on earth after this 'rapture' (Rev. 12:17). The language of Revelation also points to the male child as being Jesus himself ('who will rule all the nations with an iron scepter', Rev. 12:5; compare 2:27; 19:15) rather than the church, except perhaps by extension as his body. A 'first century interpretation' of this chapter, seeing it as describing the incarnation and death of Christ and the results for Satan's kingdom, also makes a lot of sense.

Finally, we can consider the reaping events of Revelation 14:14–20. At least the first harvest could be the rapture (Rev. 14:14–16), because Jesus seems to be the reaper and the harvest of the earth is described as ripe. The trouble is, we are well into the tribulation on a dispensationalist reading of Revelation, and in any case the imagery is not clear enough to sustain a 'worldwide disappearance' picture.

Finally, Paul's language in 1 Thessalonians 4 clearly puts the 'rapture' *after* the resurrection of all the dead believers (1 Thess. 4:15–17) and the earliest place in Revelation that may describe such an event is Revelation 20:4–6, where the martyrs are raised in the 'first resurrection' at the beginning of the thousand years.

In conclusion, a secret pretribulation rapture has to be read into Revelation, and it doesn't fit comfortably at all.

2. Can the Post-Rapture Events Described in the *Left Behind* Novels Really Be Found in Revelation?

The dispensationalist scenario is built up from a mixture of passages in the Old and New Testaments. Let's examine some of these.

The Russia-Israel war is derived from Ezekiel 38–39, where an army led by 'Gog, of the land of Magog, the chief prince of Meshech and Tubal' (Ezek. 38:2) comes from the far north (Ezek. 38:15; 39:2) to attack Israel, whose people have enjoyed a long era of peace (Ezek. 38:11). God brings heavy judgements on this army (Ezek. 38:22; 39:4–6), including fire, and there will be a feast of dead bodies for the birds and animals (Ezek. 39:17–20).

Revelation uses the language of these passages in describing two great battles at the end of its story. Revelation 19 (vv. 17, 18, 21) talks about the feast for the birds after the battle between the beast and Christ. Revelation 20 (vv. 7–9) talks specifically about 'Gog and Magog', their attack on God's city and their destruction by fire. But there are two big problems for the dispensationalist interpreter. First, the specific mention of Gog and Magog in Revelation occurs *after* the thousand years, whereas the dispensationalist needs it to be *before*. Second, La Haye and Jenkins are obliged to put it even earlier, *before the tribulation*, to fit in with their seven-year time frame, since the Israelis are said to use the wooden weapons from the invaders as firewood for seven years after the battle (Ezek. 39:9).[128] Come to think of it, burnable wooden weapons sounds a bit odd for a modern army anyway. Maybe Ezekiel had an earlier event in mind and Revelation simply uses his imagery to make its own point.

The seven-year peace treaty with Israel, initiated and then broken half way through by the Antichrist, is based on Daniel 9:27. This verse says,

> he will confirm a covenant with many for one 'seven.' In the middle of the 'seven' he will put an end to sacrifice and offering. And

on a wing of the temple he will set up an abomination that causes desolation, until the end that is decreed is poured out on him.

If this is about the Antichrist, then it requires a rebuilt and fully operational Jewish temple in Jerusalem, an article of faith for dispensationalists.[129] Perhaps Revelation 11:1 can help, since it mentions the temple in introducing the 42-month-long ministry of the two witnesses (half of seven years; though in *Left Behind*, the two witnesses are operating with just the wailing wall). But there is nothing in Revelation 11 about a treaty and no seven years – only three and a half.

Moreover, Daniel 9:27 can be plausibly read as a prediction of Christ putting an end to the Old Testament sacrificial system as part of the new covenant he was making, especially if the alternate reading of the Hebrew in verse 27b is followed, 'one who causes desolation will come upon the pinnacle of the abominable temple, until the end that is decreed is poured out on the desolated city.'[130] This reading seems to fit New Testament theology a whole lot better (cf. Heb. 8–10). These passages are difficult; I wouldn't want to base my future on interpreting them. But it seems more likely that Daniel is speaking about either his favourite enemy, the Seleucid (Greek) King Antiochus Epiphanes, who offered a pig in the temple and provoked a Jewish rebellion, or the events of Jesus' ministry, culminating in the destruction of the temple by Rome in AD 70 after a war of about three and a half years.

The figure of the Antichrist found in LaHaye and other popular writings is largely derived from Paul's 'man of lawlessness' in 2 Thessalonians 2 (though the name 'Antichrist' comes from 1 John, where it refers to false Christian teachers).[131] According to this chapter, the day of the Lord (second coming?) cannot come until this man is revealed (v. 3) and he can't be revealed until someone else is taken out of the way (vv. 6, 7). When he appears, he will set himself up as a god in God's temple (v. 4) and deceive many unbelievers by counterfeit miracles (vv. 9–11). Finally he will be overthrown by the second coming of Jesus (v. 8).

Now this seems to fit the dispensationalist schema reasonably well, including the rebuilt temple. It also seems to match the beast story in Revelation 13: beast being worshipped (Rev. 13:4), counterfeit signs (Rev. 13:13–15; though here the signs are done by a different person than the one being worshipped). But it's not a perfect match; in fact the 'man of lawlessness' may not even be a political figure; the language of Paul suggests a religious guru of some kind and Historicists identified it with the papacy.[132] And as Christians we may have reason to doubt if the Jerusalem temple (old or new) is really God's temple any more, since Jesus made its rituals obsolete (Heb. 8–10; Matt. 27:50–51; 24:1–2; John 2:19–21; 1 Cor. 3:16–17; 6:19; Eph. 2:21–22). At any rate, this passage has no mention of treaties and only the counterfeit miracles would truly reveal who the man is. It seems more likely to me that the matching passage in Revelation to Paul's prediction in 2 Thessalonians 2 is Revelation 20:8, which predicts that the devil will once again deceive the whole world and attack the saints.

From Revelation itself, the *Left Behind* series draws the judgements of the seals, trumpets and bowls, the idea of 144,000 Jewish evangelists (Rev. 7), the two prophets or witnesses (Rev. 11), the beast and false prophet (Rev. 13), the battle(s) of Armageddon (Rev. 16, 19) and the fall of Babylon (Rev. 17–18). Its interpretations of these passages make reasonable sense if you accept the dispensationalist schema of biblical prophecy, but other interpretations are possible, and even more likely, as I have argued. For example, a rebuilt New Babylon as the UN headquarters is a most unlikely interpretation of Revelation 17–18. John seems to go out of his way to show us he is talking about ancient Rome, referring to the seven hills (Rev. 17:9), a contemporary king (Rev. 17:10) and finally stating, 'The woman you saw is the great city that rules [present tense] over the kings of the earth' (Rev. 17:18).

In conclusion, the *Left Behind* series may be fascinating reading, and has perhaps helped some people give their lives to Jesus, but one has to ask if they will continue in his service once the effect of the book/movie wears off, or they come to be disillusioned with such teachings. The interpretation of Revelation found there is at best highly speculative. The long-term effect may well be disillusionment with Revelation and biblical prophecy in general, if not with Christianity itself. Certainly many young Christians I meet are a whole lot more sceptical about such uses of Revelation than the previous generation was.

Chapter 4

BAD INTERPRETATIONS

The difficulties I find in the *Left Behind* literature are not unique. Whenever people try to use Revelation to create a scenario for the future of our day, they fall into a trap, as I argued in Chapter 2. Generally such 'pop' views of Revelation are based on either or both of two ways of reading the book: the Historicist and the Futurist interpretations. But both of these are in serious danger of misreading the text. So in this chapter I want to examine how these schools of thought arose, what they say, why they say it, and where they go wrong, before looking at some alternative schools of thought about Revelation that you may never have heard of, or may have heard disparaged as 'liberal'.

The Historicist View: Revelation Forecasts World History

According to the Historicist interpretation, Revelation gives us a detailed and chronologically accurate prediction of the history of the church or world from Christ's first coming to the End.

Like the Futurist view, the Historicist interpretation of Revelation involves using a collection of selected passages from (mainly) Daniel in conversation with Revelation. For example, the ten toes of Daniel's statue vision (Dan. 2:33, 41–43) and the ten horns of his beast vision (Dan. 7:7, 20, 24) were often seen as predicting a group of ten kingdoms that would succeed the last of the empires in Daniel's vision, presumably Rome, and out of which the Antichrist would emerge (identified as the 'little horn' of Dan. 7:8, 20–21). Most Historicists see these predictions as fulfilled when independent European kingdoms came out of the ruins of the western Roman Empire and interpret the little horn as the papacy (or perhaps the holy Roman emperors). This interpretation is then carried into their reading of Revelation 17:12, which also speaks of ten horns that stand for ten kings. Quite plausible!

The Historicist view has some roots in the early church, but became particularly influential during the Middle Ages, during which many Christians were becoming disenchanted with the Holy Roman Empire, Christian kings and the papacy. It then served to undergird the anti-papal broadsides of Luther and other Reformers: during that era, it was not hard for Protestants to believe that the pope was the beast, with its overstated claims of spiritual and political authority and the Inquisition. Eventually Historicism became the dominant Protestant view for four centuries, as its advocates will never cease to remind you: they often produce an impressive list of Protestants who held this view, including even Isaac Newton.[133]

However, it could not withstand the upsurge of Futurism and dispensationalism (on the popular side) or the resurgence of Preterism[134] (on the scholarly side), and is now held by a small minority of readers, and almost no scholars. But it is not dead. It was the official position of a significant Pentecostal movement[135] in Australia for a time and also survives in the Seventh-day Adventist church and its offshoots.

How do Historicists approach Revelation? They have certain principles of interpretation:

1. *Revelation starts by predicting events in the near future of its original readers (Rev. 1:1, 3); it finishes with the last judgement and the new heavens and new earth (Rev. 20:11–21:2). Hence it is logical to assume that John's prophecy tell us in linear fashion (chronological order) the major events in between, from the first century to the very end of time.* This also means that Revelation has something to say to every era of church history. As one modern Historicist writes, 'we relativize the Bible too much if we pay so much attention to its meaning in one century only. Revelation was clearly written for all ages of the Church.'[136]

2. *A basic assumption behind this argument is that John is predicting real events in history (world and church), beginning in the early days of the church.* Historicists particularly expect to find the history of the (mainly western) church in Revelation.

3. *Everything in Revelation is symbolic code.* Historicists avoid literal readings in most cases, preferring instead to see the details of each of John's pictures as symbolizing a specific event or person in history. For example, the strange locust plague of Revelation 9 was usually seen as symbolizing the Islamic invasions of the seventh century, which conquered the Middle East and north Africa, reaching even as far as Spain.[137]

4. *Prophecies can be best understood as the time of their fulfilment draws near* (in fact, some are not understood until *after* the events predicted occur). Hence we cannot expect the early church to have had a clear picture of what the text was about, even though the text was addressed to them. Of course, this implies that we also might have got it wrong!

5. *Historicists interpret prophetic numbers in a special way. In particular there is the day to a year principle,* according to which the 1260 days of Revelation 11:3 stands for 1260 years (supported by their use of Daniel 9:24–26, which can be shown on this method to predict the first coming of Jesus Christ).[138]

6. *Historicists insist that Old Testament imagery and themes in Revelation must have a New Testament meaning or fulfilment.* So, for example, the temple of Revelation 11:1 stands for the church, in line with Paul's view that the church is the temple of the Spirit (1 Cor. 3:16, 17; Eph. 2:21, 22).

When Historicists apply these principles to Revelation, they come to two main conclusions:

- The pope is the beast (or at least the whore), whose dominance over the church and Christendom extended for 1260 years.
- We are now living close to the climax of the story, an assumption shared with many Futurists.

Now if this is the case, this approach encourages us to study the text of Revelation to look for clues about what is happening now and what is about to come upon us. Thus Historicists easily fall into the kinds of misuse of Revelation described in Chapter 2. That is, Historicists easily get involved in specific predictions, stereotyping of enemies and identifying their group as the elect. Their approach also makes them prone to date-setting, the most famous examples of which were the predictions of William Miller, which spread like wildfire across north America in the 1830s, only to be dashed when Jesus did not return as scheduled in either 1843 or 1844. This debacle led to the formation of the Seventh-day Adventist church, which cleverly reinterpreted the dates to fit their new prophetic picture.[139]

About ten years ago, an Australian publication revisited Millerism in method, if not outcome. K. Bickel's *Prophetic Time Periods in History and the Final Hour*,[140] copies of which were sent to many churches in Australia, used a complex system of date calculations to focus on 1993–1997 as an especially significant period. As it was published in 1995, it was able to claim events in 1993–94 as already fulfilling its forecasts, lending credibility to the remaining predictions. While warning that his dates are 'a guide only',[141] Bickel points to events in 1993 as beginning the final hour, including the signing of the UN Declaration on Religious Freedom and the peace treaty between Israel and the Palestinians brokered by US President Bill Clinton.[142] Bickel toyed with the idea of Clinton being the Antichrist but decided instead to limit himself to saying the US Presidency represents its spirit.[143] However, Bill Gates is definitely the 'false prophet' for promoting interactive television.[144] During the next several years, we were supposed to see a 'mark of planetary citizenship' related to inter-net buying and selling, a massive meteor collision (or two) with earth and 'the oceans of the earth . . . becoming a lifeless mass of red algae' (in fulfilment of Rev. 16:3), among other things.[145] Will Historicists never learn?

The major problems with Historicism are:

- The great variety of contradictory interpretations of history they derive from Revelation and Daniel. Adventists expect to be persecuted over the sabbath; British Israel followers expect the triumph of the British peoples; Jehovah's Witnesses expect the second coming any day now (though they have stopped saying when, after at least three false starts).

- They often focus narrowly on the West and the Middle East, to the exclusion of eastern Christianity and the other continents, for no convincing reason.
- The failure of many predictions they have derived from Revelation and the rest of the Bible. For example, the Historicist view has failed in its attempts to forecast the overthrow of the papacy by the return of Christ (Taylor and Guinness)[146] or the final overthrow of the beast in 1836 (John Wesley).[147] Even Taylor, a recent Historicist, admits that some Historicist predictions from Revelation have been 'erased' by time.[148]
- The lack of a consistent principle to control their interpretations of details in the visions.

The Futurist View: Revelation Is All about the End

Futurists writers urge that Revelation tells us mainly what will happen shortly before, during and after the second coming of Jesus.

Like Historicists, Futurists believe that John's vision contains specific predictions of events that were still in the future when he wrote it all down. Also like Historicists, Futurists have an eye on the future of our day when they read Revelation. The big difference is that Futurists see all, or nearly all, of Revelation as being *still* in the future. For most of them, the 'prophetic clock' of Revelation is stopped around the end of chapter 3, awaiting the final countdown to the public revelation of Jesus.

At some unpredictable time, which could be any day, events will start moving at speed towards this great climax, perhaps launched by the 'rapture'[149] (though not all Futurists believe in the secret pretribulation rapture). This climactic period, which for Futurists is seven years long at most, will see the terrible events of the 'great tribulation' (Rev. 7:14), the unveiling of the Antichrist or beast (Rev. 13), the downfall of Babylon (Rev. 18) and the battle of Armageddon (Rev. 16:12–16; 19:11–21). Finally

Jesus comes again and initiates the glorious millennium (Rev. 19:11–20:6).

Thus far the Futurists are agreed. However, they disagree vigorously about many of the details, such as:

Who are the Seven Churches of Revelation 2–3?

Are the messages to the seven churches prophetic words to seven real first century churches of Asia or are they *really* addressed to the church at large during seven *eras* of church history? This second way of reading them would provide a bridge between the first century and the final generation; that is, Revelation begins with its own time (Rev. 1), moves quickly through church history (Rev. 2–3), and then describes the countdown to the appearing of Jesus (Rev. 4–19).[150]

Not all writers who take this approach agree about the details, and the idea of consecutive ages of the church is often modified to fit their interpretation of church history. For example, LaHaye has the last three eras overlapping.[151] For some dispensationalists, the application of Laodicea to the modern church has served to decry modern liberal Christianity as 'lukewarm' (Rev. 3:16); it also justifies rejection of any apparently successful Christian movements, especially Pentecostal and charismatic churches that seem to be moving forward with life and vigour.

Futurists who interpret Revelation 2–3 more literally as referring to churches of John's day face a different challenge: why does the text move suddenly from the first century to the twenty-first? Often Futurists appeal to Revelation 1:19:

> Write, therefore, what you *have seen*, what is *now*, and what will take place *later*.

This verse is seen as providing the structure of Revelation: first, John's vision experience in chapter 1 ('what you have seen'), then his message to the churches of his day in chapters 2–3 ('what is now') and finally his message about the distant future in the rest of the book ('what will take place later'). This has some warrant but we must point out some problems:

1. It is not a neat division; for example, the messages to the seven churches also contain much about the future and the later chapters refer to John's present as well (e.g. Rev. 17:8, 10, 18).
2. It is a very unequal division: most of the book falls into the third section.
3. It is compatible with all interpretations of Revelation, not just a Futurist reading. How much 'later' is John referring to? Historicists also take chapters 4–22 as referring to the future. Even Preterists[152] usually take chapters 4–19 as speaking partly of the immediate future and chapters 20–22 as speaking of the more distant future.

Is the Church on Earth Or in Heaven During the Tribulation?

Obviously, the *Left Behind* series answers, 'In Heaven' – taking the call to 'Come up here' (Rev. 4:1) to be a call to heaven for the whole true church, the so-called 'rapture'. But many other Futurists warn Christians that they will have to endure the tribulation and must be careful not to take the mark of the beast. Of course, this means that for these writers, it becomes imperative to tell the reader what to look out for, so they easily fall into the mistakes described in Chapter 2.

What Sort of Persons or Entities Are the Beast, the False Prophet and the Great Whore (Babylon)?

Should we be looking at political entities (a world dictator perhaps) or religious entities (a future pope?) or both? One recent book argues strongly that it's all about Islam.[153]

How Should the Millennium Be Visualized?

Will Jesus be physically present ruling a world empire with its capital in Jerusalem, a somewhat Jewish empire with a literal new temple and animal sacrifices 'in memorial' of Christ's death? This is what most dispensational premillennialists (like Tim LaHaye) expect. Other Futurists (often called historic premillennialists) have a more Christianized or spiritual view of what it will be like. It all comes down to which Old Testament passages are seen as referring to the millennial era.

Futurists often claim that the early church (post-New Testament) held a Futurist view of Revelation. This, however, is misleading. Early Christians clearly tended to believe that most of the visions in Revelation were in the future *to them*, but this would be compatible with Futurist, Historicist or even Preterist readings now, nearly 2000 years later. For example, if the whore was the emerging papal system in the Christian church, as taught in the Historicist view, this would be *future* to the first several centuries of Christian interpreters. And there were always Christians who interpreted Revelation 'spiritually', that is, not as referring to specific historical events at all. It would be more accurate to date the rise of *modern* Futurism to the early nineteenth century.[154]

So How Do Futurists Go About Reading Revelation?

1. *They Tend to Interpret the Book as Literally as Possible*

Whereas Historicists read symbolically, not literally, wherever possible, Futurists do the reverse. For example, John F. Walvoord contends, 'terms should be understood in their ordinary meaning unless contrary evidence is adduced'.[155] So in Futurist books, you will frequently read arguments that certain visions cannot have been fulfilled yet, because no such event has (literally) happened.[156] Merrill Tenney, for instance, writes, with reference to the trumpet plagues, 'Perhaps it is safer to say that these trumpets are actual physical judgements which seem improbable because they have no antecedents in human experience'.[157] However, 'The advent of the atomic age . . . makes the idea of a cataclysmic divine intervention in the course of the physical world seem less improbable.'[158]

Futurists also tend to take the numbers in Revelation literally: so forty-two months (Rev. 11:2) literally means that! So will the ten kings of Revelation 17:12 literally rule for one hour?[159] I suppose it's just possible!

2. Thus They Tend to Interpret Visually in the Light of Current Developments

They look for modern or future events that would have *looked to John* like, say, a strange locust plague (Rev. 9): helicopter gun ships perhaps? The more popular Futurist books often talk about nuclear war, identification cards (especially implants), large meteorites hitting the earth and such like.

3. Futurists Use the End of the Book to Govern Its Interpretation

Revelation ends with the last judgement and new heavens and earth, so it must all be about 'end times'.

4. Futurists Usually See the Events Described in Revelation as Unfolding Chronologically

So the events portrayed in the seven seals (Rev. 6) will happen before those portrayed in the seven trumpets (Rev. 8), for example. As LaHaye puts it, 'With the exception of chapters 12 and 17, most of Revelation unfolds chronologically.'[160] However, in practice it is difficult to follow such a chronology exactly, and LaHaye frequently departs from it – for example, when he locates the fifth seal in the second half of the tribulation (even though it is chronologically near the beginning of John's account)[161] and when he places the prostitute of Revelation 17 in the first half of the tribulation (even though it is late in John's account) in order to fit his scenario.[162]

5. Dispensationalists in Particular Creatively Use Various Parts of the Old Testament to Interpret Revelation

This is especially the case with Daniel, but also with Ezekiel, Isaiah and Zechariah. The material from these different texts is combined to come up with imaginative scenarios for the future. Often this means taking these Old Testament passages right out of their original context and making them mean something their original hearers could not have understood.

Strictly speaking, Futurist readings of Revelation should be proof against some of the problems found in the Historicist approach: no one knows when the 'countdown' will start, so date-setting should be ruled out. For consistent dispensationalists, the rapture has no warning signs and could literally happen at any moment; therefore it is impossible to say it is going to happen in our generation.[163] But in practice, many Futurist commentators see current developments in technology, international affairs and religion as related to passages in Revelation and therefore fall into prediction,[164] demonizing groups they don't approve of, and other problems discussed in Chapter 2. In particular, they speculate about the beast and his mark, justified by the need to warn those 'left behind' or Christians going through the tribulation.

Other Problems with Futurist Approaches

Futurists tend to make the text irrelevant to its original (first century) readers. Why would the early Christians value and preserve a text that had no real message for them? Why would John write a letter to seven churches that was mainly about events they would never see?[165]

Furthermore, there are few controls on interpretation. If one visualization of, say, the mark of the beast becomes out-dated, it is easy to come up with another and convince at least some readers that 'the end is nigh'. Barry Smith had virtually named Henry Kissinger as the beast, but if he (Kissinger) dies, there will be plenty of other possibles in the wings.[166] Good interpretation therefore becomes a question of how imaginative or creative you can be.

Consequently, Futurists often seem be somewhat arbitrary in deciding which language to take literally and which to interpret as symbolic.[167] For instance, Ladd, when discussing Revelation 17:18, concludes that Babylon stood for Rome in the first century, 'but in the end time, it will stand for eschatological Babylon',[168] as Rome does not fit all the details of the prediction; for example, the prostitute sits on many waters (Rev. 17:1), which fits ancient Babylon but not Rome.[169] Nevertheless, he is not inclined to interpret Babylon literally as ancient Babylon, but rather argues that,

> John has taken over the Old Testament symbolism and used Babylon to represent the final manifestation of the total history of godless nations. The city had a historical manifestation in first-century Rome, but the full significance of the city is eschatological.[170]

In other words, take it literally only if it suits you!

Especially in dispensationalist readings, the theology of the interpretation tends to be more Jewish or Old Testament than Christian and New Testament. Thus they tend to expect the restoration of Old Testament temple, sacrifices and other institutions that seem to have been superceded in the teaching of the New Testament. This flows from the sharp distinction they make between the church and Israel.

Finally, Futurists need to explain (away) many of the time hints in the text, such as in the opening verse: 'what must soon take place' (Rev. 1:1; see also 1:3; 22:6, 10). Now admittedly, John also expects Jesus to come 'soon' (Rev. 22:7, 12, 20) and speaks of things that will happen 'later' (Rev. 1:19) or 'after this' (Rev. 4:1) But he also clearly has an eye to his own time, such as when he speaks of present political realities: 'one [king] is' (Rev. 17:10 and one 'is not' (Rev. 17:8, 11).

Conclusion

It is clear that various Historicist and Futurist readings of Revelation have led to all kinds of distortions of the text and have justified the existence of some contradictory interpretations and extreme sects. So is there a more responsible way of interpreting Revelation and applying its message to our lives in the twenty-first century? Or is Revelation so prone to misinterpretation that it is better left on the shelf unread?

Chapter 5

THE VALUE OF REVELATION

In the last four chapters, we have seen just how badly Revelation has been handled by certain readers over the centuries. As a result, many others, both Christian and non-Christian, have lost all confidence that the book is worth reading. Does it inevitably lead its readers astray into confusion or ungodly attitudes? Should it even be in the New Testament?

Such criticisms are not new. Revelation was not universally recognized as apostolic or worthy of inclusion in the emerging collection of writings now known as the New Testament. To this day, some Christian churches do not include it in their Scriptures, and others do so lukewarmly, such as the Eastern Orthodox Church, which does not include any readings from Revelation in its liturgy. The Protestant Reformers were also sceptical, at least initially, of the value of this text. And yet it survived.

Craig Koester observes that in mainline churches, many have difficulty accepting Revelation:

> The Revelation-inspired end-times antics among some Christian groups make those in the mainline wince. While not willing to deny all connection with the book, many in the mainline treat Revelation like the distant cousin who does not quite fit in with the rest of the family. They prefer not to talk much about it or invite it to family gatherings more often than necessary.[171]

Today there are new calls for Revelation to be ignored or culled from the New Testament, or at least reserved only for study by scholars of ancient culture. Mainly these derive from the misuse of the book or the values it seems to enshrine, which seem out of

step with (post)modern western thinking. Specifically, Revelation
has been attacked on the grounds that:

- It enshrines an out-dated pre-scientific worldview, full of mag-
  ical, supernatural, mythical and medieval beliefs.
- It glorifies violence, if not by Christians, at least by God on
  their behalf.
- It promotes misogyny (negative attitudes to, and stereotyping
  of, women).
- It lends itself to misuse by the 'religious right' and other forms
  of sectarian Christianity.

So was the church right to include Revelation in the canon of the
New Testament? Should Christians accept it as part of inspired
Scripture? Does it have any value today, other than as an inter-
esting historical curiosity?

I want to argue here that Revelation has value to all readers
interested in the Christian faith, not only to historians and fun-
damentalists.

1. It Inspires Christians to Sacrificial Service and Witness

Contrary to what has sometimes been thought, Revelation does
not inspire a passive attitude in Christians, along the lines of 'it's
all going to happen anyway, so why bother to work for justice or
to convert the nations.' While there is certainly an element of
determinism in the text, beginning in the first verse, with its affirmation that this is what 'must soon take place', this does not
mean that God does everything without any human involve-
ment.

On the contrary, the exhortations to the seven churches pre-
suppose that they must respond to the Spirit and overcome the
tests they face in order to inherit the future glories (Rev. 2:7, 11,
17,26; 3:5,12,21). For each church, indeed for each believer, the
promises are conditional on faithful endurance and fervent service. As Jesus puts it in one case, 'all the churches will know that I
am the one who searches minds and hearts, and I will give to
each of you as your works deserve' (Rev. 2:23).

Not only so, but also Jesus involves his followers in the battle to be fought and the victories to be won by him. Thus, although the heavenly battle between God's and the devil's angelic armies is won by Michael and his angels (Rev. 12:7–9), the text reveals that the key to victory was the faithful Christians and 'the word of their testimony' even in the face of death: '*they* have conquered him' (Rev. 12:11). Later the Lamb is revealed standing on Mount Zion with an army of 144,000 fervent disciples (Rev. 14:1–5). Again when the ten kings are defeated by the Lamb, he has others with him who are 'called and chosen and faithful' (Rev. 17:14).

Revelation is one of the great martyr texts of the New Testament.[172] The martyrs are clearly the heroes of the book. Jesus is their forerunner and model (Rev. 1:5; 11:8; 12:11). John himself is in exile because of his witness to the truth (Rev. 1:9). The individuals and churches who endure suffering are applauded in the messages to the seven churches: Ephesus (Rev. 2:3), Smyrna (Rev. 2:9–10), Antipas the martyr (Rev. 2:13), Philadelphia (Rev. 3:8–10). The cry of the martyrs for justice is heard and granted by God (Rev. 6:9–11; 19:2). They are the ones who win the battle against evil (Rev. 12:11). They stand up against the threats and violence of the beast and the allurements of the prostitute and defeat these enemies of Jesus (Rev. 13:7–10, 15, 17; 15:2; 17:14). They sing the secret new songs of victory (Rev. 14:3; 15:3–4). They rise again to rule with Christ for a thousand years (Rev. 20:4–6).

These factors have inspired suffering believers in all ages. For example, the Christians in the communist world have derived great strength and inspiration from the examples and promises of Revelation.

2. It Has Inspired Many Great Works of Christian Art, Literature and Music

Some of the more significant cultural achievements strongly influenced by, even based on, Revelation, include:

- Michelangelo's *Last Judgement*.[173]
- Handel's *Messiah*. For example, the famous 'Hallelujah Chorus' is directly based on Revelation 19:6 and 11:15, and the

oratorio ends with two other excerpts from the text of
Revelation: 'Worthy is the Lamb' (Rev. 5:12–13) and 'Amen'
(Rev. 5:14).

- Drawings and poems of William Blake.[174]
- Milton's *Paradise Lost* and *Paradise Regained*.[175]
- Albrecht Dürer's famous woodcuts on the apocalypse.[176]

Other artists and authors inspired by Revelation include
Shakespeare, Marlowe, Coleridge and Browning.

Christian hymns inspired by this book include Charles
Wesley's 'Lift Your Heads, Ye Friends of Jesus',[177] Heber's 'Holy,
Holy, Holy', Perronet's 'All Hail the Power of Jesus' Name',
Charles Wesley's 'Ye Servants of God', William How's 'For All
the Saints', and the famous 'Battle Hymn of the Republic'.[178]

3. It Makes a Valuable Contribution to Christian Theology

Revelation is a *Christian* text, in spite of doubts by some modern
commentators inclined to reduce Christian theology to the
Fatherhood of God and the brotherhood of humanity. It conveys
essentially the same message as the New Testament as a whole,
albeit with some important exceptions; for example, Paul's explanation of the gospel around the theme of justification by faith
does not appear (but neither is it found explicitly in many parts
of the New Testament, even in some of Paul's own letters) and
Jesus' teaching of loving and praying for our enemies contrasts
with the call for vengeance seen in Revelation 6:10, 16:6 and 18:20
(though it may be in the background elsewhere as I hope to show
later).

Key Christian doctrines that are taught in Revelation include:

- The uniqueness of God (monotheism; Rev. 1:8; 4:8–11; 3:2;
  4:2–3, 8–11; 7:10, 12; 10:6; 11:16–17; 14:7; 15:3–4; 16:5, 7, 9, 11;
  18:8, 20; 19:1–6, 10; 20:11; 21:2–7, 22, 23; 22:3, 5, 9).
- Creation (Rev. 3:14; 4:11; 10:6; 14:7; 21:5).
- The validity of the Old Testament (Rev. 10:7; 11:1–2, 19; 15:3, 5;
  21:10, 12; 22:6).

- The messianic office of Jesus (Rev. 1:1, 2, 5; 5:5; 12:5; 14:1; 19:15–16; 22:16).
- The historical crucifixion of Jesus (Rev. 11:8).
- The redemptive work of Jesus through the shedding of his blood (Rev. 1:5; 5:6, 9, 12; 7:14; 12:11; 13:8).
- The universal offer of salvation in the gospel (Rev. 5:9; 7:14; 14:6; 22:14, 17).
- The resurrection of Jesus (Rev. 1:5, 18; 2:8).
- The kingdom of God (Rev. 1:6; 5:10; 11:15, 17; 12:10; 20:4, 6).
- The exaltation, glorification and enthronement of Jesus (Rev. 1:6, 13–18; 2:1, 18; 3:7, 14; 5:5–13; 7:10, 17; 12:5; 14:14; 17:14; 19:11–16; 20:4, 6; 21:22, 23; 22:3).
- The second coming of Jesus[179] (Rev. 1:7; 2:25; 3:3, 11; 16:15; 19:11–21; 22:7, 12, 20).
- The general resurrection (Rev. 20:4–6, 13).
- The last judgement[180] (Rev. 6:16–17; 11:18; 16:14; 20:11–15).
- Final rewards and punishments (heaven and hell; Rev. 2:7, 10, 11, 17, 23, 26–28; 3:5, 12, 21; 7:15–17; 11:18; 14:10–11; 20:10, 15; 21:3–8, 27; 22:3–5, 12–15, 19).
- The Holy Spirit (Rev. 1:10; 2:7, etc; 4:2; 14:13; 22:17).
- The Christian church (Rev. 1:11, 20; 2–3; 5:9; 7:9; 22:16).
- The priesthood of all believers (Rev. 1:6; 5:10).
- The existence and doom of the devil (Rev. 12:3, 7, 9–17; 13:2, 4; 20:2–3, 7–10).

In fact, almost every clause of the ancient Christian creeds is to be found somewhere in this text, either explicitly or implicitly: the only exception is the doctrine of baptism.

Also the Book of Revelation adds depth and clarity to several Christian doctrines, making them more vivid and immediate. Its descriptions of the exalted Christ are unique in the New Testament and contribute to the developing doctrine of the deity of Christ; for example, Jesus is worshipped by the heavenly hosts and all creation (Rev. 5:9–14). Its description of the final judgement of every soul adds detail and colour to the teaching about this elsewhere in the New Testament (Rev. 20:11–15). And its description of the future hope of Christians in general makes its absence unthinkable!

In fact, there are several truths that are far more developed in Revelation than anywhere else in the New Testament. I have already mentioned the language used of the exalted Christ: Revelation gives us a unique picture of Jesus as he is now and as he will be in the end. Revelation also gives us a much stronger picture of the overall plan of God and the story of salvation than any other book in the whole Bible with its gathering up of the Old Testament stories and images and its portrayal of the end of the Story that began in Genesis. Revelation has a more developed angelology than any other book in the Bible, though still within the bounds of biblical teaching, without the excesses of some other apocalypses.[181] And it gives us a much clearer picture of cosmic or spiritual warfare than any other single book of the Bible, showing both the parties involved, the issues at stake, the victory already won by Christ, the role Christians are called on to play in the battle and the ultimate outcome.

4. It Makes a Valuable Contribution to Christian Worship

Revelation is the worship book par excellence of the New Testament, which otherwise contains only occasional liturgical passages, such as the songs of Mary, Zechariah and Simeon (Luke 1:46–55, 68–79; 2:29–32) and some apparent early hymns in Paul's letters (Phil. 2:6–11; 1 Tim. 3:16). It may indeed be read as a liturgical document, a worship service. Certainly it gives us a unique window on the worship of heaven.

Revelation contributes strongly to the *content* (subject matter) of Christian worship:

- God's worthiness to be worshipped due to his unique power, divinity and holiness: 'Holy, holy, holy is the Lord God, the Almighty, who was and who is and who is to come' (Rev. 4:8; see also 15:3, 4). This is not only stated propositionally but conveyed through the imagery of passages in the text (Rev. 4:2–3).
- God's worthiness due to his position as sovereign Creator and ruler of all things (Rev. 4:11; 10:6; 14:7; 19:6), a thought backed up by the repeated description of God as the one seated on 'the throne' (Rev. 3:21; 4:2, 9; 5:7, 13; 6:16; 7:15; 19:4; 21:5); he is also

called 'the Lord of the earth' (Rev. 11:4) and 'King of the
nations' (Rev. 15:3).

• Celebration of God's promises (Rev. 7:15–17; 10:7; 15:4; 19:7).
• Celebration of God's victories, which are shared with his faithful people (Rev. 11:15, 17).
• More controversially, celebration of God's judgements (Rev. 11:18;
  16:5; 18:20; 19:2, 3), based on a due appreciation of his justice.
• The person and atoning work of the Messiah, Jesus, is also central to worship as portrayed by Revelation (Rev. 1:17, 18; 5:9,
  20, 12; 12:10, 11).

Revelation's portrayal of worship in heaven also contributes to
our understanding of the *form* of Christian worship. As described
in Revelation, heavenly worship takes such forms as verbal dec-
larations (Rev. 4:8, 10, 11; 5:9, 10, 12, 13; 7:12; 11:15, 17; 15:3, 4; 19:1,
2, 5, 6), falling down before God (Rev. 4:10; 5:8, 14; 7:11; 11:16;
19:4), casting crowns before him (Rev. 4:11), use of incense (Rev.
5:8; 8:3, 4), use of musical instruments (Rev. 5:8; 14:2; 15:2),
singing (Rev. 5:9; 14:3; 15:3), shouting (Rev. 5:12; 7:10; 11:15; 12:10;
19:1), saying 'Amen' (Rev. 5:14; 7:12; 19:4; 22:20) and 'Hallelujah'
(Rev. 19:1, 3, 4, 6). It is worth asking if our church worship times
are characterized by these forms.

Finally, Revelation teaches us who Christians may legitimately
worship and which figures are illegitimate claimants to our worship. Revelation shows that God (Rev. 4:8–11; 5:13; 7:10; 8:4;
11:15–18; 14:7; 15:3, 4; 16:5, 7; 19:1, 4–6, 10) and Christ (Rev. 1:17;
5:8–10, 12, 13; 7:10; 11:15; 22:20) should both be worshipped,
which in itself makes a strong theological point. But it strongly
decries the worship of all created beings: angels (Rev. 19:10;
22:8, 9), human rulers (Rev. 13:4, 8, 12–15; 14:9, 11), Satan (Rev.
13:4) and idols (Rev. 9:20; 22:15). In fact, this is one of the central
issues in the text, the struggle over who or what to worship.

5. It Serves to Expose the Pretensions of Human Power and Religion

Whatever the precise application we make of John's evil figures –
the two beasts of Revelation 13 and the whore and beast of

chapters 17–18 – they clearly represent human powers and human religions opposed to God and Jesus Christ. They are very likely modelled on aspects of the ancient Roman world, even if applicable to later periods. The Roman Empire ruled over a vast territory around the Mediterranean Sea at the time when Revelation was written (see Rev. 13:7; 17:18). Its power was invincible (although there were occasional defeats at the hands of the Parthian empire and other enemies), as apparently reflected in the phrase, 'Who is like the beast, and who can fight against it?' (Rev. 13:4).

The Roman Empire was more than a political system. It was a vast economic entity, enhanced by the security created by Roman power (the *Pax Romana*, leading to relatively safe travel by land and sea) and Roman roads. This led to economic prosperity, especially for traders and landowners, who thus had a vested interest in upholding the empire, as portrayed in Revelation 18:11–19. But it was also a religious system, grounded in Roman civil religion (worship of the traditional pantheon of gods such as Jupiter and Venus) and increasingly also in the emperor cult, which was especially popular in the province of Asia, to which Revelation is addressed. Both of these religious forms in effect divinized the empire itself, and this was expressed in the imperial myths that created an effective propaganda.

John makes no attempt to mount an intellectual challenge to this propaganda; rather he turns to apocalyptic language and imagery, describing the empire as a wild beast (Rev. 13) or a prostitute (Rev. 17). In particular, he takes aim at its blasphemous pretensions (Rev. 13:1, 5; 17:3), its clever deceptions (Rev. 13:13–14; 18:23) and its oppressive violence towards dissidents, especially Christians, who decline to join in the civil religion (Rev. 13:15–17; 17:6; 18:24). He mocks the empire's pretensions to permanence and invincibility (Rev. 18:7–8).

John thus exposes the pretensions of human power and religion, calling instead for loyalty to God's empire ruled by Jesus Christ: 'Fear God and give him glory' (Rev. 14:7); 'Those who worship the beast and its image, and receive a mark on their foreheads or on their hands, they will also drink the wine of God's wrath' (Rev. 14:9–10); 'keep the commandments of God and hold fast to the faith of Jesus' (Rev. 14:12); 'Come out of her my people, so that you do not take part in her sins, and so that you do not share in her plagues' (Rev. 18:4).

This becomes a permanent call to Christians across the ages to put God and Christ first, not compromising with human power and religion where these challenge the supreme loyalty due to God, and not deluded or swayed by the propaganda of powerful political and religious leaders. This speaks powerfully to Christians living under anti-Christian dictatorships today, but it can also be applied to the more seductive forms of imperialism associated with nominally Christian empires such as the USA. Nationalism and patriotism are frequent rivals for the loyalty of the saints. Revelation teaches us not to rise up in violent revolution but not to be sucked in by competing loyalties to the supreme lordship of God and Christ.

6. It Stimulates and Inspires Hope in Christian Believers

Clearly one of the purposes of Revelation was to bring encouragement and hope to the poor and persecuted Christians of John's day. And from then on, it has performed a similar function in the church. Revelation shows Christians that the future is in God's hands and that the end is a good one for those who follow Jesus Christ.

Specifically, Revelation inspires Christians to hope that:

- There will be a literal resurrection of believers at the end (Rev. 20:4–6, 12–13).
- God will triumph over the forces of darkness in Christ (Rev. 12:11; 17:14; 19:11–21).
- The events promised in Revelation (such as the glories of the new heavens and earth) will certainly come to pass (Rev. 1:1; 4:1; 22:6).
- Those whose names are in the Lamb's book of life will be vindicated at the last judgement (Rev. 20:12–15; 21:27).
- Those who are suffering for Christ will receive their reward (Rev. 14:13; 15:2; 20:4–6).
- Their persecutors will be judged and punished for their cruelty (Rev. 6:9–11; 16:5–6; 18:20; 19:2).
- Christians will enjoy fellowship with God and Christ forever in the New Jerusalem (Rev. 21–22).

Such confident expectation motivates believers to endure through tough times and keep serving the Lord. It also provides a vision and hope of a just world.[182] This gives it a place in a Christian theodicy: an explanation of what God is doing about evil. Many wonder 'where is God?' when evil and injustice seem rampant all over the planet.

Revelation gives us a Christian answer:

- God is still on the throne.
- He is bringing human history to a glorious future in which evil is defeated forever.
- He is fighting with us against the powers that resist his goodness and promote injustice.
- He himself has suffered from cruelty and injustice in order to redeem his world through Jesus Christ.
- He is calling us to be involved in this great struggle, even if it costs us our lives.

Revelation provides hope and inspiration, perhaps more than any other book even in the Bible.

7. It Has a Relevant Message for Today's Readers

Is Revelation relevant today? Certainly not if it is only a historical document of what the early church expected or thought. Certainly not if its relevance depends on us successfully decoding some kind of prophetic system to work out where we are in the story. Certainly not if only the very last generation of believers can claim its promises and words of encouragement. Who knows whether we are that generation or not, since many previous generations were convinced it was them?

I believe that the relevance of Revelation today lies in applying its principles faithfully to today's church and being guided by its worldview to resist the subtle decay of Christian thinking in our postmodern world. This means we have to learn how to use the book responsibly, unlike some Christians referred to above, which is the theme of the next chapter.

Chapter 6

RESPONSIBLE INTERPRETATION

If Revelation has been seriously misused over the centuries, should we then just discard it? Or is there a responsible and valid way we can interpret this strange text? In this chapter, I try to suggest a better way to read Revelation, a way which any Christian can follow. You don't need a doctorate in theology to understand the main thrust of this book.

1. Treat It Like Any Other (Ancient) Book

This may sound surprising in the light of the previous chapters, but Revelation is not written in Martian and can be understood, if not perfectly, at least in its main ideas and structure. It's not as if we have to have a whole different set of reading skills to tackle Revelation, even though there are difficulties.

Revelation, however, is a first-century book, so we can't just read it like something published last week. We need to be prepared to do some homework:

- Read up on apocalypses, ancient Jewish texts like Revelation, in that they tell of divine revelations through angels about the future. Revelation is not a modern Futurist book or a book of esoteric codes; it needs to be read for the kind of genre it represents. Daniel 7–12 is a good example of an apocalypse. You can actually read many other apocalypses on the internet (such as 1 Enoch, which is quoted in Jude 14–15).[183]
- Read up on the historical context of Revelation. What was going on in the world of John's day, especially in the area

where these seven churches were? Hints: the destruction of Jerusalem in AD 70, the rise of emperor worship, persecution of Christians and the periodic civil wars in the Roman Empire are a few relevant events.[184]

- Read up on the nature and interpretation of biblical prophecy. A solid knowledge of the Old Testament is especially relevant for reading Revelation, especially books like Isaiah, Ezekiel, Zechariah and Daniel. But read them in their own context first.

But the normal rules for understanding any Bible book still apply.

For example, responsible interpreters enquire into the authorship, date and occasion of writing,[185] just as they would if studying a Gospel or one of Paul's letters. Unlike many New Testament texts, Revelation actually names its author, though some commentators argue about who he is.[186] The date Revelation was written, and the situation into which it was aimed, are more controversial and have significant implications for understanding it, perhaps more than for any other New Testament text,[187] but there are boundaries within which these are discussed and clues in the text itself.

For example, there are two main scenarios for the background and dating. Some scholars believe Revelation was written in the late 60s, during or just before the time the Roman emperor Nero launched a violent attack on Rome's Christians (64), which was just before the rebellion of the Jews against Rome (66–70) and the 'year of the four emperors' when the Roman Empire nearly fell apart (68–69). These events seem to be reflected in John's language and pictures. A larger number of scholars prefer a date in the mid 90s, near the end of the reign of Domitian, who was widely believed to be a strong persecutor of Christians,[188] accused of demanding worship from his subjects while still alive and regarded by some as a kind of 'second Nero'. This date is also supported by an early Christian comment by Irenaeus.[189] Either way, we can see that Revelation was written against a background of intermittent persecution, Jewish distress and general economic and political instability.

Fortunately lots of good studies are being done today on the historical context of Revelation and the New Testament generally[190] and the text itself gives us plenty of pointers, as you would expect if it was any other book. For example, there are studies which give a historical background to the speaking image of Revelation 13:15, showing that speaking statues were not unknown in the first-century world.[191] And archaeological evidence supports the claim that the emperor cult was especially strong in the region to which Revelation was addressed, which seems to be relevant to the beast passages. Some of the cities mentioned in Revelation 1–3 competed with each other for the privilege of building temples in honour of the Roman emperor.

Responsible interpreters of any text also discuss the (human) author's intention in each passage. Some postmodernist commentators criticize the idea of authorial intention, but many of them still implicitly discuss and comment on John's intentions in Revelation, even his motives for writing the book.[192] Certainly we cannot be *sure* what he intended by every phrase in Revelation, but the concept of authorial intention helps us weed out some unlikely interpretations – we can be fairly sure, for example, that John could not possibly have intended to attack the Roman Catholic Church or the modern European Union.

Another way of looking at this is to ask, what would John's original readers/hearers have understood him to mean? Remember that most of them were hearers, not readers. As printing hadn't been invented and most people couldn't read, most Christians (even in the seven churches who originally got the text) would have heard it over and over but never had the chance to examine it in detail. Thinking about what they would have understood by it also helps place boundaries around interpretation.

Of course, at this point someone will ask, what about the Holy Spirit's role in the writing process? Couldn't he have intended a lot more than John or his original hearers understood? And the answer is, of course he could, and probably did. But the only way we can understand what the Holy Spirit was saying is through the actual words of the book as they were understood by its first readers and listeners. If we abandon this test, all bets are off and we can use the text anyway we like. I hope the earlier chapters of this book have convinced you of the results of doing that!

We follow these sorts of reading rules automatically with other old books, such as the Gospels or ancient Roman writings. Let's not get sucked into treating Revelation like something totally different.

Responsible readers also give attention to the literary features and structure of a text. We should treat Revelation as a whole book, just as we would any other Bible book. This means studying the structure, the literary features, the development of the plot, etc. It demands that we compare Revelation with other biblical literature: not just Daniel (the most popular choice), but other Old Testament prophecy (such as Isaiah), Paul (since Revelation is structured as a letter), and the Gospels (since Revelation is a prose narrative about Jesus); early books like Genesis and Exodus are also very relevant. Revelation should also be compared with non-biblical literature of its own era. For instance, as mentioned previously, the study of apocalyptic writing, of which Revelation is an example, will help us avoid many interpretive mistakes, such as the picture book method of interpretation used by some Futurist writers.

Responsible readers respect the literary context of individual passages.[193] For example, speculations on the meaning of '666' (Rev. 13:18) must be justified by placing this verse in the context of the whole of chapter 13 and 14, not to mention the way John uses numbers generally.

2. Interpret Literally But Carefully

What I mean by this is that we should take John at his word, not necessarily agreeing with him, but not reading extra difficulties into the text that aren't really there. For example, John tells us he was on the island of Patmos (Rev. 1:9) where he had a strange vision of Jesus one Sunday (Rev. 1:10) and was instructed to send his text to seven churches in Asia Minor (Rev. 1:11). Why shouldn't the reader take this at face value? Why try and read hidden meanings into these plain statements? Why 'spiritualize' the seven churches so that they are *really* seven eras in church history, for instance?

This may seem surprising, but many commentators who most loudly claim to be literal are really only *literalistic*. What I mean is this: they advise us to look for a future army of, say, helicopter gun ships, in order to take 'literally' the language of Revelation 9, but refuse to take seriously John's claim that 'the time is near' (Rev. 1:3) or that his intended audience is seven churches in first century Asia Minor.

Of course, the principle of literalism does not help us much with understanding, say, the meaning of the beasts in Revelation 13; it only assures us that John *really saw such figures* in his vision. No interpreter that I know of takes these beasts 'literally' in the sense of expecting wild animals like this to arise and rule the world (shades of *Planet of the Apes!*). But reading literally helps us avoid importing allegorical meanings where none are required to make sense of the text.

But literal reading must also be careful. At times the text is clearly symbolic or uses codes. The most famous example is the 666 (Rev. 13:18), where the text challenges us to 'calculate the number of the beast'. This seems to allude to the ancient practice of gematria, where numbers could stand for letters: Roman numerals used the letters of their alphabet. History has shown that it isn't hard to get almost anyone's name to equal 666 if you use the right mathematical formula. So what can we do with this case? It seems to me that responsible interpreters would not be too dogmatic about their interpretation. However, we must also assume that John's original readers would have had a better understanding of his meaning than we could possibly equal nearly 2,000 years later. Hence very early interpretations are more likely to be right. This means that the leading candidates would be Nero or the Roman Empire generally (from the word Lateinos).[194]

Another brake on too literal a reading would be the recognition that imagery is meant to be just that: it appeals to the imagination and is not meant to be taken apart and interpreted as a code or allegory. So, for example, the description of the 'great prostitute' in Revelation 17:4 paints her as a Roman prostitute, but it would be fruitless to ask, what does the golden cup in her hand 'stand for'? It's more likely to be just part of effect that John is creating by word pictures, giving the feel of luxury and debauchery which he wants us to associate with the Roman world. On the other hand, in the same chapter, some of the other details about the woman, or more accurately the beast she rides, do stand for specific geographical, political or historical features; for instance, 'the seven heads are seven hills on which the woman sits' (Rev. 17:9). We need to let John himself, and his angelic helpers, be our interpreters here.

There is also need for care when we read passages that use language that can be deceptively 'normal'. For example, John's use of numbers: are there exactly 144,000 people sealed as described in Revelation 7:1–8? Are there precisely 12,000 from each Israelite tribe? The figures seem too rounded to be taken literally; compare the statistics in the Old Testament for example, as in the first census in Numbers (Num. 1–3). And one tribe is missing (Dan), a fact which has given rise to all sorts of elaborate theories. It seems more reasonable to suppose that John is using these numbers figuratively. Similarly, is John predicting a period of exactly 1,000 years after the imprisonment of the devil (Rev. 20:1–7) or does this figure simply mean 'a long time'? The use of such a phrase elsewhere in the Bible would suggest the latter (compare Ps. 90:4 and 2 Pet. 3:8).

There are many cases like this where John's language *could* be taken literally but it would make better sense not to. A few examples. 'A fourth of the earth' (Rev. 6:8) is affected by sword, famine, plague and wild animals; does this mean a quarter of the whole planet or a quarter of the known world of John's audience or even a quarter of the land of Israel (the Greek word for 'earth' can be translated 'land')? Similarly, what would it mean if 'a third of the sun was struck' (Rev. 8:12)? Could anything survive? And could blood literally rise as high as horses' bridles for 300 kilometres (Rev. 14:20)? How many people or animals would need to be killed to produce such a blood bath? Might it not be more likely that John is using hyperbole or some kind of symbolic language?

3. Explore the Relationship between Revelation and the Rest of the Bible

The early church placed Revelation in its canon of Scripture. That means not only that they recognized it as an inspired book from God, but that they saw it as part of a larger whole, what we call the Bible. This suggests that we should not isolate Revelation for special study as if it was totally different and unrelated to the teaching of the rest of Scripture. Revelation makes a special contribution to the message of the whole Bible. But it cannot be understood well in isolation from the rest of the Bible.

For example, Revelation never quotes directly from the Old Testament, and never uses phrases like 'according to the prophet', but it alludes to the Old Testament more than any other New Testament text.[195] Moreover, these allusions are to many books of the Old Testament, not just Daniel. Check it out with the cross-references in a good reference Bible. Some of the very significant references are to Genesis 1–3 (especially in the promises to the seven churches and the descriptions of the New Jerusalem), Exodus (e.g. the plagues of Egypt and the judgements of Rev. 16), Psalms (especially Ps. 2, which John alludes to at least four times), Isaiah (e.g. the New Jerusalem, new heavens and earth and the lake of fire), Ezekiel (Gog and Magog, the resurrection scenes, the call narratives), Joel, Zechariah and even the Song of Solomon (compare Rev. 3:19–20 with Song 5:2–7).

Revelation also has allusions to other parts of the New Testament.[196] You may have noticed the parallels between Jesus' Olivet Discourse (Mark 13; Matt. 24; Luke 21) and the seals passage (Rev. 6); what conclusions follow from this? In places it seems that Revelation is describing imaginatively what other passages in the New Testament speak of more propositionally (compare Rom. 2:5–11 with Rev. 20:12–15 on the final judgement and 2 Pet. 3:7–13 with Rev. 20–21 on the 1,000 years and the end).

Moreover Revelation seems to be written deliberately as the 'last' book of the Bible. It seems to be explicitly trying to finish the story found in Scripture, especially in its allusions to the early chapters of Genesis in Revelation 21–22.[197] If this is so, it has some powerful implications: John believes that the Bible is a single book with a common story of creation-fall-redemption-consummation, not just a collection of useful stories and teachings. We can use Revelation to help trace that story, an epic war story-cum-romance, of God and his people.

Perhaps the main conclusion that comes from studying Revelation in the context of the whole Bible is that we come to see it as a book of fulfilment. Rather than seeing it as predicting the future (though it does that to some degree), we realize that it claims to show how Jesus fulfills earlier prophecies and promises of God – a theme of much of the New Testament.

For example, the first salvation promise in the Bible is Genesis 3:15. God says to the serpent, who has just led Adam and Eve into sin:

> And I will put enmity between you and the woman,
> and between your offspring and hers;
> he will crush your head,
> and you will strike his heel.

Clearly this is promising the demise of the devil. But who is this offspring of the woman and how does this promise come to pass? Revelation gives us an answer, though not in theological language. In Revelation 12, we see a woman giving birth and a huge scarlet dragon waiting to devour her child. The dragon is identified as the ancient serpent of Genesis (v. 9). The child is identified as the promised Messiah:

> She gave birth to a male child, who will rule all nations with an iron scepter (Rev. 12:5a).

This is a reference to Psalm 2, which speaks of God's Anointed One (Messiah) being opposed by the kings of the earth but, nonetheless, receiving the nations as his inheritance:

> You will rule them with an iron scepter;
> You will dash them to pieces like pottery (Ps. 2:9).

The dragon is unsuccessful in his attempt to devour the Messiah; the child is exalted to God and his throne (Rev. 12:5b). Instead the dragon loses a heavenly war with Michael and his angels and is thrown out of heaven (Michael is the champion of Israel in her battle with ungodly powers, according to Daniel 10:13, 21; 12:1). Thus the Messiah wins:

> Now have come the salvation
> and the power and the kingdom of our God
> and the authority of his Christ (Rev. 12:10a).

But how? Was it just that the godly angels were more numerous or physically stronger? Did the Messiah have a more powerful military force than the empires sponsored by the devil? No:

> They overcame him
> by the blood of the Lamb
> and by the word of their testimony;
> they did not love their lives so much
> as to shrink from death (Rev. 12:11).

This victory was won by the crucifixion of Jesus Christ and delivered by the faithful witness and suffering of his followers. The victory over the serpent has already been accomplished; the promise has already been fulfilled. And yet there is still a future element. The schemes of the dragon continue (chapters 13–19), the sufferings of God's faithful witnesses continue, the dragon is not yet locked up. As is a common theme in New Testament eschatology, it is a case of 'already' but 'not yet'. We have the victory but we still have to fight on!

These are the kinds of studies we can do with Revelation and the Old Testament, in the light of the rest of the New Testament, once we abandon the false trails of Historicism and Futurism.

4. Study the Theology and Worldview of Revelation

Revelation is much more than a chronology of past, present or future events. It's a book with a message, a book that aims to *do* something.[198] It's also not just a book about eschatology (the study of the so-called 'end times'), but it has a specific perspective on God, Christ, the Holy Spirit, angels and salvation, to mention just a few topics. We need to explore Revelation's theology just as much as Paul's or Luke's.[199]

Revelation, like the rest of the Bible, also comes with an implicit worldview; that is, a particular way of envisaging reality, truth, history, the cosmos, human beings, etc.[200] This is one of the reasons we have trouble with it today: its worldview is not ours! But this is one way where Revelation becomes extremely relevant today. I want to choose my words carefully here. I do not believe that we can just accept the worldview of Revelation, or the Bible generally, as our worldview *uncritically*. To do that would mean complete rejection of modern science, for instance. But I do believe that Revelation has a significant role in correcting or adjusting our worldview.

Christians are constantly in danger of uncritically adopting the worldview of the surrounding culture. For example, today we are tempted not to take the Bible's language about evil spirits or the devil seriously. And we are under pressure to tone down the language about hell found not only in Revelation but in the teaching of Jesus, replacing it with a more acceptable position to a generation influenced by postmodernism, for example. This is not just a theological or exegetical issue: it goes to the heart of our worldview, in this case the way we see God, humans, ethics, law and history. Revelation can play a vital role in ensuring that we do not lose this perspective and in correcting those aspects of our worldview that are 'out of sync' with the way that God thinks as revealed in Scripture.

In conclusion, there is a right way to read Revelation, a way that tends to avoid extremes and the traditional misuses described in earlier chapters. But part of this requires us to think carefully, why did John write Revelation?

Chapter 7

WHY DID JOHN WRITE REVELATION?

Before we look at how Revelation is relevant to us in the twenty-first century, we need to ask about its purpose and impact on the time when it was first written. Why did John write this text and what did he hope to achieve? Some recent commentators are convinced that he had ulterior, namely *political*, motives. He was motivated either by envy of Rome, and the desire to see it come tumbling down, or he was trying to win an intra-church struggle with the Christians represented by terms like 'Nicolaitans' and 'Jezebel'. There may be some truth in these assertions: certainly John was against Rome (especially its imperial cult) and opposed to the Nicolaitans and Jezebel – he makes no secret of that! But Christians might still give him the benefit of the doubt and suspect that he had good reason for his point of view, even that he was led by the Spirit to take such stands.

So why then did he write?

1. On Instruction

The simplest answer, if we take his words at face value, is that he was *told* to write down what he saw and heard (Rev. 1:11, 19). Of course, this assumes he really had the vision(s) he describes. Some recent interpreters deny this, but largely (I think) because their worldview doesn't allow for such possibilities. It is true that others made similar claims, as in the Jewish apocalypses referred to earlier, but I am prepared to trust the Holy Spirit and the church when it recognized this claim as valid by accepting Revelation into the canon of Scripture.

However, such a simple answer, while (I believe) true, doesn't quite exhaust the question, for two reasons. First, we must then ask, why was he given the vision and told to write it down and send it to those seven churches? What purpose did the Holy Spirit have for leading him to write these words? Can we find an answer to this? And second, while I believe John really did see and hear the things he reports in Revelation, the finished product, the text we now read, is his production as well as that of the Spirit. It was written in his language. It was encapsulated in a letter to these seven churches. It incorporates his descriptions of the situation he was in when he wrote (Rev. 1:9–10) and some of his reactions to what he saw (Rev. 1:12; 5:14; 7:14; 10:4; 17:6). So it is still legitimate to ask, why did John do that?

2. Support for Persecuted Christians

This is more the traditional answer from commentators who don't try to read modern times into Revelation. They read about the intense persecutions undergone by early Christians, particularly at the hand of the Roman Empire, and conclude that John wrote to support and encourage them with the hope that they would be released and resurrected to reign for a thousand years. But this view has been much criticized in recent years. Several scholars, for example, have questioned whether there was such intense persecution at the time when Revelation was written. Nero's attacks on Christians were limited to the city of Rome; why would believers in Asia Minor need support during that period? And the earlier view of Domitian as a power-mad dictator who insisted on being worshipped as Lord and God, and thus attacked Christians who refused to conform, is being challenged (or at least modified) on historical grounds.[201]

Nonetheless some version of this view is still likely to be correct, in my opinion. John writes to a particular region and its churches. He is encouraging them in particular. And he himself states that they are undergoing opposition and persecution, at least locally and intermittently. The Ephesians have 'endured hardships for my name' (Rev. 2:3). The Smyrnans have experienced afflictions, poverty and slander, most likely from the local Jewish synagogue (Rev. 2:9). The Christians in Pergamum have lost one of their leaders, Antipas, as a martyr (Rev. 2:13). Those in Philadelphia have also faced Jewish opposition, even pressure to deny Christ (Rev. 3:8, 9) and have had to 'endure patiently' (Rev. 3:10). Summing up, four out of seven churches are experiencing some degree of pressure or opposition from outside.

But more significant is the suffering they are *about* to face. It seems that John is trying to prepare his churches for a new round of persecution to come, of which the less consistent pressure they have experienced so far is just a foretaste. So the Smyrnans are told, 'Do not be afraid of what you are *about to suffer*', and warned of imprisonment and other persecution 'for ten days', even possible death (Rev. 2:10). The church in Pergamum may have experienced its worst, but is reminded that their city is the site of Satan's throne (Rev. 2:13), which suggests more trouble ahead. The Philadelphians will be rewarded with exemption 'from the hour of trial that is *going to come* upon the whole world to test those who live on the earth' (Rev. 3:10, emphasis added). This may be a summary of the trials forecast in the remainder of the book. Certainly John sees major, and worldwide, persecution about to hit the churches. Hence they do need encouragement in order to stay faithful under such pressure.

3. Correction of Problems within the Churches

Recent commentators have emphasized the words of rebuke and correction given to the Christians within the seven churches. Perhaps one of the emerging forms of Gnosticism had been invading some of these churches, a similar situation to that faced by the churches envisaged in 1 and 2 John or, say, 1 Timothy, Jude or 2 Peter. Or perhaps John is the extremist attacking a more tolerant form of Christianity resembling the freer norms of Paul.

Certainly the messages to the churches spend more time on internal problems than external threats. For instance, the church at Ephesus is praised for rejecting false prophets and the Nicolaitans, but accused of forsaking their first love. The church in Pergamum is said to be too tolerant of a Nicolaitan minority among the believers. The church of Thyatira is tolerating the false prophet Jezebel and her followers, who are about to face punishments from Christ. The Christians in Sardis are dead, or at least sleepy, and need to wake up spiritually. And the church in Laodicea is lukewarm and complacent; these Christians need to realize how needy they are and repent, allowing Jesus to live among them again.

However, if this is the major reason for the text as a whole, we have to find a connection between these issues and the remaining chapters, which seem to function well as encouragement for persecuted saints but less obviously as correction for the sleepy, cold, lukewarm or excessively tolerant churches criticized in chapters 2–3. This brings me to what I think is John's, or the Holy Spirit's, main purpose.

4. Encouragement to Fervent Discipleship

One of the common elements in the messages dictated to the seven churches in Revelation 2–3 is the promise to those who 'overcome' (or conquer, the Greek word is *nikaö*, related to the goddess of victory *Nike*, after which the popular sports shoes are named). Whatever problems the Asian Christians were facing, whether it was external threats or internal ones (dissensions, moral challenges, false prophets, declining commitment), the challenge was for them to stand up, face the challenge and win the victory! If we examine closely both the praise and the blame handed out by Christ in these messages, it is clear that what he is looking for is fully committed and fervent disciples.

For example, Christians are praised for good deeds (2:2, 19), hard work (2:2), perseverance (2:2, 3, 19), enduring hardship (2:3, 9; 3:10), remaining true to Jesus under pressure (2:13; 3:8), love (2:19), faith (2:19), service (2:19) and purity (3:4). They are criticized for forsaking their first love (2:4), tolerating false teaching, especially of a form that is lenient towards eating food sacrificed to idols and sexual immorality (2:14, 20), spiritual torpor (3:1–3), lukewarmness (3:15–16) and complacency or pride (3:17). They are urged to repentance (2:5, 16, 21; 3:3, 19), faithfulness (2:10), perseverance (2:25), obedience (3:3), self-awareness (3:17), earnestness (3:19) and discerning concentration on their real needs (3:18):

> I counsel you to buy from me gold refined in the fire, so that you can become rich; and white clothes to wear, so that you can cover your shameful nakedness; and salve to put on your eyes, so that you can see.

If we consider the qualities represented by these exhortations, we can see that John (or the Spirit) is very concerned that the believers in Asia live lives characterized by strong commitment, high moral standards and humble service.

In particular, he is calling on these Christians to be full of fervent love for the Master that will withstand both pressures and allurements from the surrounding culture. Thus even good 'performance' (in terms of rejecting false prophets and serving faithfully) does not count if it does not issue from their 'first love' (2:4), seemingly a reference to their initial conversion and emotional response to their Saviour, with possibly an allusion to Jeremiah 2:2, where God reminisces, 'I remember the devotion of your youth, how as a bride you loved me'. The Ephesians are exhorted, 'Remember the height from which you have fallen', and warned that they will lose their lamp stand if they don't repent (2:5). As in the Gospels (Matt. 10:37), Jesus demands to be loved above everything else.

Similarly, the Laodiceans are about to be spat out since they are lukewarm (emotionally detached), even though seemingly prosperous both materially and spiritually. They are blinded by their apparent blessings and need to go through a process of self-humbling and earnest repentance (3:17–19). Jesus loves them but they are shutting him out (3:19–20). In a probable allusion to the Song of Solomon, Jesus is portrayed as standing outside the church knocking on the door to gain entrance to his beloved (compare Song 5:2). The love that he wants is thus compared to the erotic relationship between young lovers. Such a fervent discipleship will enable Christians to overcome and win the rewards he promises.

This theme continues in the rest of the text. For instance, the overcoming Christians win the victory over the dragon, their accuser, 'by the blood of the Lamb and by the word of their testimony; they did not love their lives so much as to shrink from death' (12:11). In other words, they are the kind of believers envisaged in chapters 2 and 3. They love Jesus more than their own lives (souls), just as Jesus demands in the Gospels (Matt. 10:37–39; 16:24–26; Mark 8:34-38; Luke 9:23–26; 14:26–35; 17:33; John 12:25). They are the ones who will thus remain faithful under the persecution of the beast (13:8–10; 14:12) and resist the seductions of the prostitute (18:4). They receive the reward at the end, which is reserved for overcomers (21:7) and those who 'wash their robes' (22:14), a reference to spiritual life and purity (3:4; 7:14; 19:8), and withheld from those who are 'cowardly' or who compromise with the ungodly culture (21:8; 22:15). The message is very clear: only fervent and committed disciples of Jesus will make it through the trials encountered by the church.

The literary structure of Revelation sends the same message to the seven churches. It seems that the reference to the Song of Solomon is no accident because the storyline of Revelation resembles that of a romance. This is clearest at the end: the story ends with a wedding between the Lamb and the Holy City (19:9; 21:2, 9). The bride stands for the faithful overcoming believers since they alone have the right to enter the city (22:14), a message with significant Old Testament foundations (read Hosea, Jeremiah 2–3 and Isaiah 5:1–7, for example). The bride is contrasted with the prostitute, whose love affair with the beast ends in disaster (Rev. 17) and from whom true believers must dissociate (18:4). The sexual language is quite explicit in the description of the prostitute and her ruin (17:4, 16).

Revelation thus begs to be read (at least in part) as a romance story. Jesus as the future husband seeks the total fervent love of his followers (Rev. 2–3). The future bride faithfully follows him under incredible pressure from the beast, and in spite of deception from the false prophet. She resists becoming like the prostitute, who carries on an illicit affair with the beast. She is like the 144,000 virgins who bear his name and devote themselves totally to the Lord (14:1–5). After a long time of great testings and vicissitudes, she receives her reward, being married to her Lover. Many of Revelation's readers would see this element in the story, because they had heard or read love stories before, either in the epics, comedies and romance novels[202] of the Hellenistic world or in the (Old Testament) Scriptures[203] and other Jewish literature.[204] If John told the story well, they would see themselves as being called to be part of that faithful bride consisting of all those who truly loved and served Jesus Christ, no matter what the cost.

Summing up, then, John sought to prepare and encourage the Christians of Asia for their forthcoming great persecution and ongoing cultural pressure by pointing them back to the same Jesus that is described in the Gospels, who is both incredibly attractive and incredibly demanding. But we must not imagine that he only wanted the believers to survive the onslaught and pressure. The word 'overcome' or 'conquer' suggests that he wanted them to triumph over the culture.

5. Strategy to Conquer the Empire

A number of recent scholars have pointed out that John's attitude to the Roman world and government seems at odds with the encouragement to submission found in Romans 13:1–7 and 1 Peter 2:13–17 and the generally positive view of Roman authority found in Acts. Either John is a sectarian, society-rejecting extremist or the situation he is facing differs from these other texts.

This kind of argument depends on an overly simplistic understanding of the other Christian texts mentioned. It is true that Paul urges submission to authority and asserts that existing authorities serve at God's appointment (Rom. 13:1–6), but he also preaches Jesus as Messiah and Lord (as in Rom. 1:4), both terms with potentially revolutionary implications: in a Roman worldview, Caesar alone was Lord and claims to messiah-hood could lead to Jewish revolts against Roman power. Romans also launches a strong critique of the Greco-Roman society of the first century, which it declares to be exposed to God's wrath (Rom. 1:18–32).

1 Peter is written to an audience in the eastern empire facing strong persecution (1 Pet. 1:6; 2:12, 20, 21; 3:14, 17; 4:1, 12–19; 5:8–10), which he traces ultimately to the devil (1 Pet. 5:8). This needs to be 'resisted' (1 Pet. 5:9). While he never countenances

political resistance to the authorities, Peter's rationale for sub-mission is partly so that the Christians can live down their critics (1 Pet. 2:13–15): clearly the believers are being verbally attacked and need to prove their innocence by their good lives (1 Pet. 2:12, 15; 3:15–16; 4:4, 15, 16). He also exalts Jesus above the Roman rulers and sees obedience to Jesus as the purpose of the Christian life (1 Pet. 1:2, 3, 14; 3:15). Like John, he emphasizes the impor-tance of love for Jesus as the motivation for faithfulness (1 Pet. 1:8) and calls on the believers to disassociate themselves from the ungodly culture around them, which he sharply criticizes (1 Pet. 1:18; 2:11–12; 4:3–4). He sees the Christians as an alternative soci-ety within the empire (1 Pet. 2:9), living in tension with it.

Neither Paul nor Peter encourage their readers to live like the Greco-Roman society. They are just as 'rejectionist' as Revelation when it comes to idolatry and immorality. And Acts presents a mixed view of the Roman authorities. They protect the early Christians against Jewish attacks at times (as in Acts 17:5–9), some Roman officials show interest in the faith (Acts 10–11; 13:6–12) and many of them act fairly towards Paul (Acts 19:23–41); certainly they protect him from assassination at the hands of certain Jews (Acts 21:31, 32; 23:12–35; 25:3–5). But often they fail to intervene when mob violence is stirred up against Christians (Acts 13:50; 14:5, 19; 17:13; 18:12–17), sometimes even support such violence (Acts 16:19–24), fail to respect Paul's citi-zenship rights (Acts 16:37; 22:23–29), and fail to give him justice after he is taken into custody in Jerusalem even though they know he is innocent of the Jews' accusations against him, because it is politically expedient to please the Jewish leaders (at least partly) by keeping Paul 'out of circulation' (Acts 24; 26:31, 32).

So what is John urging on *his* readers? Is he deliberately incit-ing them to hatred of the Roman Empire, maybe even to rebel-lion? Very clearly not. The resistance to Rome which he proposes is at most passive, expressed in such terms as 'endurance', 'perseverance' and 'faithfulness' (Rev. 2:3, 10; 3:8, 10; 13:10; 14:12). Yes, his imagery of Rome is negative and sharply drawn (Rev. 13, 17) and he clearly expects God's judgement to come on those who persecute Christians and live in self-indulgent luxury (Rev. 15, 18). But he is only projecting what he and his readers were already experiencing in a measure from Jews, Romans and others (Rev. 1:9; 2:9, 13) and what the future looked likely to bring as Christianity became more of a threat to the powers-that-be of the empire (Rev. 2:10; 3:10; 6:9–11).

So what does he want his readers to *do*? Clearly he wants them to endure and persevere faithfully in their Christian life, as I argued in the last section of this chapter. But there is also a note of conquest in Revelation. As we saw, the believers are meant to be conquerors. So what are they supposed to conquer? Is it just temptations, persecutions and the general pressure of the surrounding culture? Or is there a bigger vision?

Let's look at some key themes. First, Jesus is portrayed as a conquering hero: 'the ruler of the kings of the earth' (Rev. 1:5), the one coming on the clouds (Rev. 1:7), with a double-edged sword coming from his mouth (Rev. 1:16; 2:12, 16; 19:15), having authority over the nations (Rev. 2:26, 27; 12:5; 19:15). He is 'the Lion of the tribe of Judah' who has triumphed (Rev. 5:5), who has purchased people for God from every people (Rev. 5:9; 7:9), who rides out to battle and conquest on a white horse (Rev. 6:2 perhaps; 19:11). The leading people of the empire are deadly afraid of him (Rev. 6:15–17). He becomes the final possessor of the kingdom of the world (Rev. 11:15; 12:10), overcomes the ten kings of the beast (Rev. 17:14), and then the beast and false prophet (Rev. 19:19, 20). He has the title 'King of kings and Lord of lords' (Rev. 19:16). John tells the tale of a long, bloody and costly war, but the outcome is not in doubt: Jesus wins! At the end, it is Jesus, not the beast or the dragon, who is in charge and reigns for a thousand years (Rev. 20:4, 6). If we can put this in terms of John's day, Jesus conquers the Roman Empire.

But he does not do it alone. Associated with him in all his victories are the overcoming, conquering believers. They have become a kingdom (Rev. 1:6, 9; 5:10). They are also promised a share in his triumph: authority over the nations (Rev. 2:26, 27), a seat on his throne (Rev. 3:21), reigning on the earth (Rev. 5:10). With their Leader they win the victory over the dragon (Rev. 12:10, 11) and the beast (Rev. 15:2; 19:14?) and the ten kings (Rev. 17:14). They rise to share his thousand-year rule (Rev. 20:4–6). So they also conquer the empire.

But how is this to be done? What strategy does John envisage for this conquest? Clearly not armed resistance: that would be

both suicidal and against the principles of Christ. But also not just
a passive waiting for God to act in judgement, though God clearly
is expected to act powerfully and decisively for His people. No,
John has quite a clear picture of what will bring this seemingly
invincible empire down and replace it with a Christian one. And it
is arguable that the early church put his strategy into action and
gradually wore down the empire, though the outcome was not
quite what they perhaps expected when the emperor Constantine
bowed the knee to Jesus Christ in 312.[205]

If we read carefully, we can begin to see what the God-given
strategy to conquer the world included. It required faithful witness to Jesus, even at the cost of martyrdom. This is what John
himself was doing at the time he was exiled to Patmos 'because
of the word of God and the testimony of Jesus' (Rev. 1:9) and he
was following the example of Jesus himself (Rev. 1:2, 5). Some of
the Christians in Asia are commended for the same faithfulness
(Rev. 2:3). Some have already suffered for their testimony (Rev.
2:9, 13; 6:9), one even died (Rev. 2:13) and worse suffering could
be expected (Rev. 2:10; 6:11; 11:7–10), though some might be
spared (Rev. 3:10).

But this witness would conquer. As Revelation 12:11 proclaims,
'They overcame him by the blood of the Lamb and by the word
of their testimony; they did not love their lives so much as to
shrink from death.' This victory is a joint effort: Jesus' death gives
him the right and position to rule the world (Rev. 1:5; 5:5, 9, 12)
and the witness of the saints gives them the right to rule with him
(Rev. 1:6; 2:26, 27; 3:21; 5:10; 20:4–6; 22:5). John expects the church
to overcome opposition and persecution and conquer the empire,
and in a way that is what happened over the next few centuries!
Even Tim LaHaye asserts that 'the Church reached its greatest
numbers in proportion to world population during this period of
persecution.'[206]

Let's explore the strategy a bit further. How would this conquest
happen? Once again it is important to note that John does not call
on Christians to use political or military means (as these are nor-
mally understood) to grasp power. While his text is full of violent
language and imagery of war, he never suggests that Christians
use violence. In fact, even the Lord conquers by suffering (Rev.
5:5–12) and his sword comes only from his mouth (Rev. 19:15).

The first part of this strategy is *separation or non-compromise.* John is clear in his insistence that Christians have nothing to do with idolatry or immorality, in other words they are to be an alternative society, not participating in key aspects of the surrounding culture. This is why he urges the churches to have nothing to do with their members who advocate a softer line towards the Greco-Roman polytheistic culture. Christians needed to be distinct in order to have a definite message to the Roman world. And this challenge was largely taken up by Christians after John's death: they refused to take part in all aspects of the surrounding culture that had anything to do with idolatry, immorality or cruelty, including gladiatorial fights, theatre and offering incense to statues of Caesar.

Second, they are to conquer by *prayer.* While John sees a world under God's sovereign control, so that the things he foresees '*must* soon take place' (Rev. 1:1), he is not a total determinist. For example, the seven churches addressed in chapters 2 and 3 have a real choice about their future: '*If* you do . . ., I will . . .'. And each believer has the opportunity to become a conqueror. But also in the world of this text, God hears and answers prayer. One of the ways John portrays this is by the use of Old Testament symbolism. For instance, in Revelation 8:1–5, there is a pause in the action between the seven seals and the seven trumpets, during which incense is offered before God in heaven 'with the prayers of all the saints' (v. 3; see also 5:8), and God replies with signs in the earth and its atmosphere (v. 5). The text is implying that the prayers of believers are part of the mix that determines what will happen next.

Third, by giving their lives in *uncompromising witness* to Jesus as Lord, they appeal to God's justice. When innocent people suffer and die at the hands of ungodly foes for their faith in Jesus, this creates a cry for justice. So when the fifth seal is opened (Rev. 6:9), John sees the souls of these martyrs and hears their cry, 'how long . . . before you will judge and avenge our blood on those who dwell on the earth?' (Rev. 6:10), not so much a cry for personal revenge as for justice, in a tradition that goes back to the very first biblical martyr, Abel (see Gen. 4:10). And justice will be done. This is why Christians believed that their witness for Jesus even to death had value and power (Rev. 12:11). In Revelation, this principle is given as the main reason for the final plagues and the fall of Babylon: 'It is what they deserve!' (Rev. 16:6).

But this is not just a case of strict justice, the law of exact consequences. Revelation does not urge the martyrs to pray for their persecutors or forgive them (as demonstrated and urged by Jesus and Stephen, Matt. 5:44; Luke 23:34; Acts 7:60). But it does agree with the rest of the New Testament in seeing a redemptive factor in martyrdom. For instance, in Jesus' case, the heavenly chorus sings, 'you were slain, and by your blood you redeemed people to God from every tribe and language and people and nation' (Rev. 5:9). But in relation to the Christian martyrs, both Jesus' blood and their own deaths are said to overcome the devil, particularly in relation to his accusations against God's people (Rev. 12:10–11).

How much can we draw from this? Certainly Jesus' death is unique in its significance and power. But the Christian witnesses who likewise lay their lives on the line for the truth could perhaps be said to help redeem the world, at least in the sense of applying the power of that unique death to the society to which they bore witness.[207] In other words, their innocence mitigated against the injustice of their persecutors, strengthening the legal case for the salvation of those persecutors or their associates.

God always acts, and can only act, according to his own principles of justice. Thus it took the death of the innocent Christ to enable the world to be justly saved from their guilt and bondage to the accuser, and it also took the death of many innocent witnesses to obtain the release of the societies that resisted the gospel. Perhaps this sounds too speculative, but certainly Revelation posits a link of some kind between the suffering of martyrs for Jesus and the victory of his cause.

6. Apologetic for Christianity

Not many interpreters of Revelation see it as having any ability to communicate beyond the boundaries of the Christian church. Indeed, it was clearly aimed mainly at the seven churches of Asia. However, these believers did not exist in a vacuum. They had only been Christians for a short time, having previously been attached to Judaism or Greco-Roman religions. And they were under pressure from both Judaism and the Greco-Roman religious traditions. Clearly they needed a way of interpreting their world, and the pressures they were facing, that moderated the tensions between their new faith and the apparent realities pressing on them on all sides.

This meant that they needed (among other things) a way of connecting their hopes, traditions and aspirations as Jews or Greco-Romans with the truth of Jesus. This was also necessary so that they could communicate their new faith to their non-Christian neighbours and defend themselves against the criticisms those neighbours would bring against Christianity. This is why a group of Christian writers arose after the time of Revelation known as 'apologists'; not that they were apologetic about what they believed but they were trying to defend their faith and commend it to non-Christians.

I believe Revelation has a similar purpose. John wants to strengthen the intellectual support for the new believers' faith and make their faith seem plausible because it connects with their hopes and traditions as former Jews or Greco-Romans. He also wants to contend against the propaganda war being waged by the Roman Empire, which was aimed at securing the allegiance of every person in the empire to Caesar and the civic deities to whom the empire owed its existence (so it was believed). To those steeped in such a faith, the call of Christian preachers for people to stop worshipping the traditional gods and to place Jesus above Caesar looked somewhat treasonable; in fact many pagans argued that Christianity was a threat to the order and stability of the Roman world. Whenever disasters came, they were inclined to blame the Christians; after all, they had persuaded a considerable number of people to stop worshipping the gods, and the gods would naturally be angry. Perhaps this is why John carefully portrays disasters as being controlled by his God for the very purpose of persuading people to turn from idols to the one true Creator.[208]

How does Revelation go about this task of making Christianity seem reasonable and real within a Roman-controlled world? John doesn't construct a rational argument. Rather he appeals to the imagination (a bit like someone today making a movie to argue a

case). And he uses imagery from his vision to connect the new
faith to the legitimate hopes, dreams and traditions of the first-
century world.

For example, Jews and Jewish believers were strongly interested in the future hope of Israel. Since the sixth century BC, they
had been living under the rule of successive Gentile empires
(Babylon, Persia, the Greeks and the Romans), with a short period of somewhat disappointing independence under the
Hasmoneans (167–63 BC). Was this all that God had for them? Or
would there be a return to the glory days of David and Solomon?
And what would be the future of Jerusalem? Depending on when
Revelation was written, Jerusalem and its temple was either
about to be destroyed by the Roman armies or was lying in ruins
as a result of that attack. Had God finished with Israel and
Jerusalem? This is, of course, a very controversial issue today,
and in some respects it is the central question that divides dispensationalists from other Christians. In the light of the
Holocaust and the re-establishment of the state of Israel, it is also
a very politically relevant question.

Revelation's contribution to this debate seems to include four
main ideas. First, that Jerusalem is still important to God. It is still
in some sense 'the holy city' (Rev. 11:2). But second, it is a city
under judgement for rejecting both Jesus and the prophets (Rev.
11:7–10), thus it is named 'Sodom and Egypt' (Rev. 11:8), which
spells doom! Third, in the midst of judgement, at least some of the
people would turn to God (Rev. 11:13) and thus there would be a
faithful Israel alongside the unbelieving one: this is suggested by
the 144,000 of the twelve tribes in Revelation 7 and the episode of
the mother figure in chapter 12, whose children 'keep the commandments of God and hold to the testimony of Jesus' (Rev.
12:17).

Finally, there is a future for Jerusalem: there will be a 'New
Jerusalem' (Rev. 21:2), a truly holy city that fulfills the promises of
the prophets of Jerusalem as a world capital (Rev. 21:24–27; read
in the light of passages such as Isaiah 2:1–5; 54:1–17 and 60:1–22).
However, this will be a Christian city, not exclusively for ethnic
Jews but reserved for those whose names are in the Lamb's book
of life (Rev. 21:22–22:5). By portraying Jerusalem in this way, John
seeks both to address and *adjust* the hopes of his Jewish readers.

What about Gentile believers? Greeks and Romans valued stability and order. Their legends placed great store on order as opposed to chaos. Order was supposedly maintained by the pantheon of gods whose favour was solicited in their traditional religious ceremonies. One ancient myth, the combat myth, told of a challenge to the legitimate gods by a monster figure and its defeat by a champion of the pantheon. This story had already been taken up by some of the Old Testament authors and reshaped to tell a Hebrew story of God's triumph over his enemies. The Roman Empire had adapted it to its own use, portraying Caesar as the champion of order and guarantor of the *Pax Romana*. John's vision in Revelation 12 seems to allude to the same story, but in this case it is Jesus who is the champion and the empire is the chaos monster. In this way, John does two contrasting things: he endorses the desire for order and provides a new story to challenge the pagan one and replace it with faith in Christ.

In similar ways, he builds on the Greek ideal of the city state by announcing the downfall of 'Babylon' and its replacement by the 'New Jerusalem', he replaces faith in the stars with faith in the one who rules over the cosmos and he re-describes the goddess Roma as a prostitute by contrast with the true 'bride' of the Lamb. In all these ways, he imaginatively demonstrates the superiority of Christianity over its rivals.

Conclusion

All these reasons I have suggested for the production of Revelation are based on the assumption that it was first of all written to the people of its day, beginning with the specified audience of seven churches in Asia. This seems to me to be an essential basis for understanding the book, as it would be for understanding other books of the New Testament and any other (ancient or modern) literature. However, if Revelation is part of the Bible, this implies that it also has a message for us in the twenty-first century. This message is what many writers who made the mistakes identified previously were trying to find. So how then can we relate this ancient book to our own times?

Chapter 8

THE RELEVANCE OF REVELATION TODAY

The danger of some uses of Revelation, especially among academics, is that the text becomes great historical source material but of little value or relevance for us today.

A Preterist interpretation of Revelation, which relates it almost exclusively to the ancient world, can make Revelation apparently irrelevant (or at least difficult to apply) to today's readers. On the other hand, the Futurist reading only makes the text relevant at the risk of daring (and so far false) speculation about forthcoming events 'predicted' in Revelation. The Historicist view allows for parts of Revelation to be directly applicable to every generation, but again at the risk of speculative (and usually mistaken) identification of where we are on the time-line of predictive prophecy as found in this text.

Is there a better way? A use of Revelation that speaks to all generations, not just the first and the last of the Christian era, yet respects the original context and intention of the text and the results of good scholarship. After all, if you believe, as I do, that Revelation belongs in the canon of New Testament Scripture, then it has a message for all believers, not just its original hearers and readers. Thus the promise in the opening words still holds good today:

> Blessed is the one who reads aloud the words of this prophecy, and blessed are those who hear, and who keep what is written in it, for the time is near (Rev. 1:3).

Reviving an Alternative Reading Strategy

The way of reading Revelation that I am proposing is a variant of the spiritual or Idealist interpretation. In this reading model, the text is not anchored *exclusively* to any particular event or period of history, whether the days of the early church and Roman Empire or the very end of the age. Rather it speaks to all eras of Christian history because the spiritual forces and issues Christians face tend to be the same in all centuries, though wearing different dress according to the specific circumstances of any particular period.

So, for example, the beast is constantly arising afresh out of the sea, attempting to eliminate or cow true believers by violence and intimidation, and often in alliance with false religion, as graphically portrayed in Revelation 13. In John's day, the beast was probably the Roman Empire (if not a specific emperor, such as Nero or Domitian), the core issue was the imperial cult and worship of Roman civic deities, and the empire's allies were perhaps the priests of the cults in the province of Asia, where the seven churches, and to some extent the Jewish synagogues, were located. The whore represented the alluring seductive face of Greco-Roman culture that tried to entice the churches to compromise. For John and his fellow Christian leaders, this was a 'life and death' struggle for the survival and eventual triumph of the gospel, a struggle that continued for centuries until the time of Constantine.

Then the situation changed conpletely, or seemed to. The church was now favoured and privileged by the Roman authorities who had just been trying to destroy it. No doubt the Christians of that day were grateful to God for relief from persecution and the opportunities presented by their new position of political power. But what arguably happened was not the thousand years of peace promised in Revelation 20, though the Catholic and Orthodox Churches did become quite dominant for a millennium. Rather there was a new challenge in which the persecuted Christians were gradually morphed into new persecutors of non-compliant spiritual groups, both pagans and 'heretical' Christians, and the influx of half-converted Romans into the newly favoured churches caused new forms of lukewarmness, compacency, conmpromise and spiritual decline; just what some of the seven churches of Revelation 2–3 had been warned about.

In fact, by the late Middle Ages some Christians were starting to identify the papacy, or specific popes, as the beast. Now strictly speaking, John could not have intended the imagery to refer to the pope when he wrote down his vision in the first century. But the spiritual force represented by this image might well have taken such a scandalous form in order to survive and make a new comeback: after all the beast of Revelation 13 (vv. 3, 14) is described as a master of comeback from apparently fatal setbacks. Thus when believers of the late Middle Ages, and the Reformers, started to see the Roman Catholic institution as the beast, or the whore, they were not entirely wrong, because it was exhibiting at least some of the characteristics of these figures: political, economic and religious power, claims to supernatural validation, immense wealth, and systematic persecution of (dissident) Christians and others.

But does this mean the Catholic Church is the beast or the whore? Not really. It was captured by this spirit for a time, and perhaps some of the results are still in Roman Catholicism (and need eradicating), but true believers gradually overcame this enemy, even as they had the original Roman Empire. However, the beast takes on new forms and will constantly do so until the final victory. In the twentieth century, the beast was probably manifest most strongly in totalitarian dictatorship, whether fascist or communist: look for the combination of great wealth, power and persecution of Christians. Now it might be represented by violent militant Islam, though some prophetic commentators point to the modern West (or specifically the USA) – both might be true. Perhaps in today's world, the beast is represented by militant Islam and the whore by the decadent West: both in their own way are a threat to the commitment of professing Christians.

In this way of reading Revelation, it speaks a fresh and vital word to every generation of believers, warning against compromise and complacency, and urging us to faithful life and witness for Jesus.

Some Case Studies

How might this reading approach work? Will it take us anywhere or does it open up the possibility of reading whatever we like into the book of Revelation? Let's look at some of the more difficult passages. In these I will ask some questions suggested by the arguments in this book and offer possible answers.

Revelation 9

This is one of the most obscure passages in the whole book in my opinion. Not surprisingly, then, some of the interpretations offered are particularly 'creative'. But let's see if we can't get some light on it.

1. What is the context?
This is the fifth (and sixth) trumpet, part of a series of seven (Rev. 8:2–11:19) that threaten increasing disasters on the world. The first four all affect one third of the world (Rev. 8:7, 9, 11, 12). Then three woes are pronounced in advance of the last three trumpets, two of which are described in chapter 9. Straight after chapter 9, we have the story of the seven thunders and the little book, followed by the two witnesses of chapter 11, before the final trumpet sounds, announcing the kingdom of God and the final judgement (Rev. 11:15–18). So chapter 9 represents the penultimate stage of these ascending disasters.

2. What is the overall impact on the imagination?
The picture conveyed by this passage, it seems to me, is one of intense suffering, largely caused by warfare. Here we have two armies, one perhaps more spiritual in nature, but in both cases people suffer intense torment, such that in the first case they want to die (v. 6) and in the second case they do die by the millions (v. 18; notice again the one-third proportion).

3. What key details stand out?
- The overall control of God comes out in phrases such as 'he was given' (v. 1), 'they were allowed' (v. 5) and 'release the four angels' (v. 14).

- God's purpose seems to be to bring the world to repentance; however, the survivors are stubborn and refuse to change their ways (vv. 20–21). Maybe this is a parallel to the Exodus when God warned Moses that Pharaoh's heart would be hardened, in spite of similar disasters.
- Spiritual (angelic) forces take a big part in these scenes: e.g. a fallen star (v. 1), the angel of the abyss (v. 11), and the angels at the Euphrates (vv. 14, 15).
- Human agency is also significant among both the sufferers and at least the second army.
- John's tendency to divide all humanity into pro- and anti-God groups is very evident. God's people are protected from the locusts (v. 4) and the unbelieving survivors are adamant in their refusal to repent (vv. 20–21). No middle ground seems possible.

4. What allusions to Scripture or the Greco-Roman world seem evident?

The locust plague, which may even be symbolic of a human army, seems to allude to the Old Testament book of Joel, where an army of locusts (possibly standing also for a human army) is sent into Israel as a punishment by God, with the goal of causing the people to repent. It is followed by restored prosperity and then by a somewhat more eschatological scene including a final war.

The location of the four angels at the Euphrates river would bring up several connotations for John's audience. The Euphrates was the traditional eastern boundary of the Roman Empire, beyond which were the often dangerous Parthians (they defeated Roman armies several times and even conquered Judea for a short period in the first century BC). It was also the direction from which invaders of Israel often came.

Some of the scenes in this chapter are reminiscent of the destruction and suffering that formed part of the Jewish-Roman war of AD 66–70, particularly during the siege of Jerusalem.

5. What was John's purpose in telling these scenes?

The primary message seems to be: choose to be on the right side – God's! Those who have his seal on their foreheads are protected even in the midst of disasters. The rest become hardened and seemingly unable to repent. So the point is, repent while you have time, of the idolatry and other sins of the Greco-Roman society (vv. 20–21). War may well break out with great suffering and loss of life.

As I argued earlier, John wants to urge his audience to a very 'full on' surrender to Jesus Christ. This part of his story should help motivate them towards such a commitment, including trust in God's protection.

However, the allusions to Exodus and Joel warn the reader that not everyone will repent, including many Jews, and these unrepentant ones will oppose and persecute the church. But this is God's way of delivering his people into their destiny, just as he used Pharaoh's stubbornness as part of his strategy to rescue Israel from Egyptian bondage. So the believers should not be scared but trust God.

6. How does it apply to us today?
The same kinds of struggles face us today. Warfare of various kinds, epidemics and natural disasters all come on the world, often without much warning.[209] God promises to protect his people at such times, even if they die. But there is no ultimate safety for those who do not follow Christ (compare Ps. 91 and Matt. 10:26–39).

These wars are permitted by God. Christians are not necessarily called to take part on one side or the other. We are on God's side only: this is the only safe place to be!

Revelation 17

The picture of the great prostitute 'Babylon' and her alliance with the beast from the abyss, which ends in disaster, is one of John's most striking images. Commonly it is interpreted as standing for one of these three entities:

- The city of Rome, beneficiary and sometimes victim of its empire: Rome was partly destroyed several times in the 60s during the fire under Nero and the civil strife after his departure.
- Jerusalem, judged for her unfaithfulness to God and destroyed with great bloodshed in AD 70.

- The post-Constantinian Roman Catholic Church, the 'adulterous' church that allied itself with the Roman emperor and its successors.

1. What is the context?
The fall of Babylon has been anticipated several times before in the story (Rev. 14:8; 16:19) but now it is given centre stage after the episode of the seven bowls of God's wrath (Rev. 16) which portray the final devastation of the beast's empire. Immediately after the two chapters on the fall of Babylon we read of the marriage of the Lamb; seemingly there is a contrast between an immoral and tragic sexual alliance (the beast and the prostitute) and a holy marriage (the Lamb and his bride).

2. What is the overall impact on the imagination?
Largely this is a horror story. The picture of the prostitute is gaudy and repulsive: she is wealthy and highly decorated but morally repugnant; in particular, she is not only drunk and immoral, but she is drunk with the blood of the witnesses to Jesus. But her end is even more horrific:

> And the ten horns that you saw, they and the beast will hate the whore; they will make her desolate and naked; they will devour her flesh and burn her up with fire (Rev. 17:16).

Many ancient readers would be reminded of times when cities were invaded and their populations subject to rape, destruction and massacre. This is followed by a lengthy lament over her fate in chapter 18.

3. What key details stand out?
- The sexual language and imagery: whore (vv. 1, 5, 15, 16), fornication (vv. 2, 4), impurities (v. 4), nakedness (v. 16).
- The alliances portrayed here between the whore and the beast and the kings of the earth (vv. 2, 3, 12, 13, 16, 17).
- The very negative language used of the woman in relation to God: blasphemous (v. 3), abominations (vv. 4, 5), drunk with blood (v. 6).
- The prominence of the whore: sexual partner of the kings (v. 2), sitting on the beast (v. 3), clothed in colourful finery (v. 4),

named 'Babylon the Great' (v. 5), source of evil ('mother of whores and of earth's abominations', v. 5), seated on seven mountains (v. 9) and on many nations (v. 15), ruling the kings of the earth (v. 18).

- The description of the beast, which is both similar to and different from the beast of chapter 13.
- The lengthy, but enigmatic, interpretation of the vision offered by the angel (vv. 7–18).
- The apparent allusions to the political situation in the first century world (vv. 9–10, 12, 18).
- God's control and ultimate victory (vv. 12–14, 17).

4. What allusions to Scripture or the Greco-Roman world seem evident?

The most obvious parallels from the Hebrew Scriptures have to do with the spiritual adultery committed by Israel and Judah when they turned aside from loyalty to God to pursue other deities or alliances with ungodly nations (or both; they were often connected). In particular, two passages in Ezekiel stand out. In Ezekiel 16, God portrays himself as a just husband who adopted 'Jerusalem' when she was a naked baby, brought her up and then married her, only for her to offer herself to a string of lovers as a prostitute (except that she paid them rather than the reverse, vv. 31–34), specifically the Egyptians (v. 26), Assyrians (v. 28) and Chaldeans (v. 29). These lovers would come and strip her and violently destroy her (vv. 37–40).

Then in Ezekiel 23, the prophet tells the story of two sisters, Oholah and Oholibah, representing Samaria and Jerusalem.[210] They both lusted after lovers apart from the Lord; in Oholibah's case, the Assyrians (v. 12) and Chaldeans (that is, Babylonians; vv. 14–17). These lovers would come and destroy her as part of God's judgement on her for her disloyalty to him (vv. 22–35): the language has striking elements of sexual violence like the passage in Ezekiel 16 and Revelation 17:16.

Historically these warnings were fulfilled when the Chaldeans (Babylonians) destroyed Jerusalem and its temple in 587 BC. Also similar to Revelation 17 is the description of Jerusalem as a whore in Ezekiel 23:40. Such parallels have led many commentators to identify the whore of Revelation 17 as either first-century

Jerusalem (which met a similar fate to the invasion of 587 BC at the hand of the Romans in AD 70) or the Catholic Church, since only a people belonging to God or Christ could be accused of adultery against him. However, this whore is accused only of prostitution, not of disloyalty to an existing relationship with God.

Allusions to the city of Rome are also evident in this passage. The description of the prostitute seems like a caricature of the goddess Roma (who represented the city and was often worshipped in Asia as a representation of the empire). The seven mountains on which she sits seem like an obvious allusion to Rome's seven hills (v. 9) and she is called the ruling city over the kingdoms of earth (v. 18). Possibly the successive kings of Revelation 17:11 refer to successive Caesars. Moreover, the disasters that befall the city seem to be an apt allusion to the way the city of Rome was burned and sacked by several emperors and Roman armies.

5. What was John's purpose in telling these scenes?
At least two reasons seem to stand out. First, he wanted to distance his hearers/readers from a power that they might find alluring, by showing its true nature and imminent fate. The beautiful city (Rome or Jerusalem) represented a worldly and immoral system that subverted those who entered into relationship with it and persecuted the saints and witnesses to Jesus. Not only so, but it was doomed to destruction. Thus John's explicit purpose (stated in 18:4) was to encourage his readers to come out of her, not necessarily in a physical sense (though this did happen in the case of Jerusalem in obedience to Jesus' words, see Luke 21:20–24), but certainly in terms of their ultimate loyalty.

Second, in line with his purpose throughout the book, John was pointing his readers not only *away from* Babylon the prostitute but *towards* their true lover (Jesus Christ). This becomes very clear after the chapters on Babylon's fall when the marriage of the Lamb is announced (19:7–9), but it is indicated in chapter 17 when he describes the war between the prostitute's allies and the Lamb and his allies (v. 14). Two things stand out here. First, readers would have to take sides in this imminent conflict: either for the ten horns or for the Lamb. They are being urged to be 'called and chosen and faithful' (v. 14). Second, the Lamb will win this battle: he will *conquer* them (using one of John's key words from the seven messages in chapters 2–3). So the Christian reader or hearer is being motivated to stand up against the allurement of Babylon and on the side of Christ, the winning team.

6. How does it apply to us today?
Applying this chapter to our twenty-first century situation depends on making some kind of comparison between the prostitute Babylon and forces that seek to draw us into a similar compliance with worldly values and powers. What forces today draw us away from Christ by their wealth, apparent security, promise of pleasure and worldwide influence? Post-industrial capitalism springs to mind, though it does not *persecute* Christians like the prostitute did. Nevertheless, its offer of unlimited pleasure and affluence (as in the pornography industry, movies, music industry, travel, etc.) are poised to draw Christians away from their 'first love'. This reminds us that the world (unredeemed culture) is an enemy of faith.

Some More General Comments

Let's consider more broadly how Revelation applies to our lives in any century. Here are a few thoughts among many we could take.

First, Revelation is an encouragement to fervent, uncompromising, radical discipleship of Jesus and a warning against lukewarm, self-satisfied, smug, complacent Christianity or Christians who tolerate sexual immorality or flirt with paganism in any form. This is made abundantly clear in the messages to the seven churches (Rev. 2–3) and then reinforced throughout the story of the book.

Second, it is an encouragement to Christians suffering persecution today (the greatest number in history) and thus an exhortation to us all to stand with them.

Third, it encourages Christians to have a very 'black and white' view of the spiritual life and the nature of the world. According to Revelation, every person in the world is either a follower of Jesus or a follower of the devil's kingdom. They are either sealed by God or by the beast. They are in the Lamb's book of life or headed for the lake of fire. While there is an understandable reaction against 'insider/outsider' or 'bounded set'[211] thinking in modern evangelical Christianity (often for good reasons), Revelation reminds us that ultimately everyone is on one side or the other of a cosmic war. There is no neutral ground here.

Fourth, Revelation warns all people that there are eternal consequences of our choices in this life. There will be a last judgement. All people will end up in the New Jerusalem or the lake of fire forever. Again, there has been an understandable reaction against too strong an emphasis on heaven and hell in Christian preaching, and a desire to emphasize the blessing of God in this life. This reaction has been needed. But things have gone too far in the other direction. Too many western believers are embracing extreme 'health and wealth' teachings. Others are trying to combine Christianity with belief in a sanitized form of reincarnation. Many theologians are abandoning the doctrine of eternal hell in favour of annihilationism[212] or ultimate reconciliation.[213]

Now it is possible to overemphasize the negative strands in Revelation. Some scholars have rightly called us to stress its positive expectations: the hope of an unaccountably huge international redeemed humanity (Rev. 7:9), the takeover of the world by God's kingdom (Rev. 10:15), the universal worship of God (Rev. 15:4), the downfall of oppressive regimes like Babylon (Rev. 18), the rule of the martyrs with Christ (Rev. 20:4–6), the redemption of human culture in the New Jerusalem (Rev. 21:26) and the hope of a future world free from injustice and ecological distress (Rev. 21:1–22:5).

But the book strongly stresses the dark side too, the unpopular stuff like eternal conscious torment (Rev. 14:9–11), the lake of fire (Rev. 20:14) and the exclusion of the unrighteous from the New Jerusalem (Rev. 21:27; 22:15). Thus it functions as a protest against such dangers as materialism, sexual indulgence, an over-easy tolerance of 'other religions' and neglect of the needy and oppressed, and a call for repentance and worship of the one true God alone (Rev. 14:6–7).

Conclusion

Revelation has always been a controversial text. Perhaps it always will be. This is no bad thing: controversial books can stir our thinking and challenge our assumptions. Thus the Spirit can shake us up and stir us up to become more fervent and faithful as followers of Jesus Christ.

For this reason, it is dangerous to proclaim that we have this book 'under control' because we have either explained it fully or explained it away! Better to let it unsettle our neat theological systems and interpretations. Better for it to challenge our tendency to compromise or complacency. Far better for it to challenge us to dangerous loyalty to Jesus, even at the cost of our lives.

We live in exciting but dangerous days. Maybe Jesus will come soon, maybe not. Certainly things are changing as never before and we can't really know where it will end, at least in the short term. The challenges of global warming, AIDS, Islamic terrorism, nuclear weapons, poverty and famines and various kinds of injustice (including rampant persecution of Christians in many places) are immense. Postmodernism and revivals of non-Christian religions are posing new intellectual challenges to the faith. However, the opportunities are also huge and more people are coming to Christ than ever in history. These are not days for the faint-hearted. Maybe Revelation will come into its own as the special book for these times.

Chapter 9

WHAT ABOUT THE MILLENNIUM?

One of the defining features of Christian eschatology and interpretation of prophecy is the passage in Revelation 20 about the
1,000 years during which Satan is locked away and the martyrs
reign with Christ. Christians have generally interpreted this in
several different ways, partly depending on how they relate the
1,000 years to the second coming of Jesus.

1. Premillennialists

Premillennialists, as we have seen, expect Jesus' second coming
to be before the 1,000 years. They teach that Jesus will come
again at the time of the final battle (Rev. 19:11–23) and institute
his personal reign on earth as the penultimate stage of God's
program, the messianic kingdom. As Satan is locked away during this time, it will be a time of unprecedented blessing, right-
eousness and prosperity. All true Christians will be raised from
death to rule with Jesus, so the earth will contain both ordinary
mortal humans and immortal saints with spiritual bodies. It
would seem to be a bit like Jesus' post-resurrection relationship
with his disciples, except that this time we will have millions of
resurrected Christians mingling with ordinary people. What
happens to those who follow Christ and die during the 1,000
years is unclear. Premillennialists insist that the same (Greek)
language is used of the first resurrection (vv. 4–6) and the subsequent general resurrection (v. 5), so they must both denote a
physical resurrection as taught by Paul and other apostles
(1 Thess. 4; 1 Cor. 15).

Dispensational premillennialists expect Jesus to rule visibly from a literal capital city, Jerusalem, in which there will be a literal Jewish temple with animal sacrifices offered as memorials of the cross.

Historic premillennialists (including Historicist interpreters of Revelation) usually speak in more spiritual terms of Jesus' millennial rule and do not necessarily envisage a literal throne or temple in a literal city.

Both groups believe that there will be a final rebellion at the end of the 1,000 years, stirred up by a newly released Satan, and then Satan will be removed permanently to the lake of fire while in the last judgement those whose names are not found in the Lamb's book of life are sentenced to join him there.

A literal reading of Revelation 20 in the light of a chronological view of Revelation as a whole may tend to support this view as follows:

- Final battle with the beast and second coming
  of Christ   Rev. 19:11–23
- Capture and imprisonment of Satan for 1,000
  years   Rev. 20:1–3
- Resurrection of true Christians, including
  'tribulation saints'   Rev. 20:4–6
- Rule of Christ with the saints for 1,000 years   Rev. 20:4–6
- Release of Satan at the end of the 1,000 years   Rev. 20:7
- Satan conspires to raise an army to attack
  Jerusalem   Rev. 20:7–9
- Satan's army destroyed by fire   Rev. 20:9
- Satan consigned to the lake of fire forever   Rev. 20:10
- Final general resurrection   Rev. 20:11–13
- Final judgement of all people (excluding the
  resurrected saints)   Rev. 20:12–15

However, there are problems with a premillennial reading of Revelation 20.

- It assumes a linear chronological reading of Revelation in spite of evidence in the text of 'recapitulation', that is the parallels between different stages of the narrative, so strong that they suggest John is re-telling the same events in different ways. Compare, for example, the seven trumpets and the seven bowls. Note how the final end seems to come over and over again before breaking though to the new age of the kingdom of God (Rev. 6:12–17; 7:6–7; 11:15–18; 16:15–21; 19; 11–21; 20:7–10). This suggests perhaps that John is re-telling the story of the end from different perspectives. Other interpretations are possible, but certainly this feature of Revelation needs accounting for.

- It depends on reading Revelation 19 as describing the second coming of Jesus. This may be correct but is not stated in the text.
- Revelation 20:1–3 pictures Satan as being imprisoned by an angel, not Jesus, as we might expect if he has just come again in glory.
- According to Revelation 20:4, it is particularly the martyrs who come to life and reign with Christ. Other Christians are not mentioned. This is strange if this is the final resurrection of all believers taught by the rest of the New Testament. It is particularly strange on a dispensationalist reading, in which these martyrs are those 'left behind' at the rapture. They are apparently heroized above the body of Christ.
- The millennial period is hard to visualize. Certain Old Testament passages are imported into the scenario to 'flesh it out' by some premillennialists, but it seems confused, especially the picture of immortal humans and mortals living together on earth.
- Other New Testament passages portray a general resurrection of both Christians and unbelievers at the same time (the second coming and the last judgement) rather than two events a thousand years apart (see Acts 24:15; John 5:28–29). Some do speak only of the resurrection of believers, however (1 Thess. 4; 1 Cor. 15), without mentioning unbelievers. No other text speaks of two general resurrections or describes a resurrection only of non-believers.
- Other New Testament passages portray a last judgement where Christians and others are separated (such as Matt. 25:31–46), but the premillennial reading requires that Christians are not present (except perhaps as judges) in the

final judgement. This leads them to posit a separate judgement of Christians to account for passages like Romans 14:10–12 and 1 Corinthians 3:12–15. Several passages picture the final judgement coming immediately after the second coming of Jesus (Matt. 25:31–32; 2 Thess. 1:7–10), not 1,000 years later.

- The idea of a 1,000-year messianic reign on earth followed by another Satanic rebellion seems somewhat bizarre, even pointless. Why would Satan be removed and then let out again?
- Some forms of premillennialism (usually dispensationalist) create very negative expectations of ever increasing wickedness and church decline leading up to the second coming. This can become a self-fulfilling prophecy, especially these days in western countries. Premillennialism has a tendency to pessimism.

2. Amillennialists

Amillennialists see the present Christian era as represented by John's 'thousand years'. Thus there is no future millennium awaiting us; rather the second coming will immediately lead to the general resurrection of all people and the last judgement, in which both Christians and unbelievers will participate and be divided into their respective destinies, as taught elsewhere in the New Testament (Matt. 25:31–46; 1 Thess. 4:14–5:3; 2 Thess. 1:6–10; Acts 24:15).

Amillennialists see the binding of Satan and the first resurrection as the results of Jesus' atoning work in his cross and resurrection, appealing to such cross-references as John 12:31 ('now the prince of this world will be driven out', in the context of Jesus' coming death, v. 33), Matthew 12:29 (the binding of the strong man, in the context of Jesus' deliverance ministry), Luke 10:18 ('I saw Satan fall like lightning from heaven', in the context of the mission of the seventy disciples) and Colossians 2:15 (at the cross Jesus 'disarmed the powers and authorities'). In this era, Satan is not finally destroyed, but restricted 'to keep him from deceiving the nations' (Rev. 20:3); thus the nations (or Gentiles) can come into the kingdom of God, as happens in Acts.

The first resurrection, then, in which the martyrs come to life and reign with Jesus, must refer to *either* Jesus' own resurrection (which is indeed the first and the model for all, as 1 Cor. 15:20 points out) in which the martyrs of old participated (Matt. 27:52–53) and into which Jesus' martyr followers are drawn at death (2 Cor. 5:2–4; Rev. 11:7–12) or a spiritual resurrection for all Jesus' followers, as explained by passages such as John 5:24 (the believer 'has crossed over from death to life'), Ephesians 2:4–6 (God 'made us alive with Christ . . . and . . . raised us up with Christ and seated us with him in the heavenly realms'), Romans 5:17 (we 'reign in life' through Jesus).

Either way Jesus and his followers are reigning now. Jesus' current rule is indicated in Matthew 28:18; Acts 2:33–36; Ephesians 1:20–22 (here the church is involved too) and Rev. 1:5 (where Jesus is seen as 'the ruler of the kings of the earth'). Some key passages for this debate include 1 Corinthians 15:24–28 and Revelation 5:10. 1 Corinthians 15:24–28 speaks of Jesus defeating all his enemies, including finally death itself, and then handing over the kingdom to God the Father: 'he must reign until he has put all his enemies under his feet' (v. 25; alluding to Ps. 110:1). Is this reign in the future, *starting after* he comes again, or now, *concluding with* his second coming? It could be read either way, but it certainly makes sense that Jesus is ruling now and his reign culminates in the final defeat of death (v. 26) when he comes again and the saints rise again forever (vv. 21–23) and the messianic kingdom is rolled over into the eternal reign of God (vv. 24, 27–28). Psalm 110 clearly speaks of the Messiah ruling 'in the midst of' his enemies while functioning as a priest in the order of Melchizedek, which is seen as fulfilled by Jesus *now* in passages like Acts 2:34–36; Heb. 1:13; 5:6; 7:17–8:2.

Revelation 5:10 shows that the destiny of Jesus' people is to be 'kings and priests' who 'will reign on the earth' (see also 1:6). This is seen as in the future for John, though based on Christ's cross (5:9). See also the promises to overcomers in Revelation 2:26–28 and 3:21. These passages clearly show a future dimension to the rule of the saints, but they seem to be referring to the New Jerusalem rather than the 1,000 years, where 'they will reign forever and ever' (Rev. 22:5). The fact that there is a future dimension to the kingdom of God does not rule out the reality of a present rule of Jesus and his saints.

The final rebellion of the unbelieving world, led by a newly free Satan (Rev. 20:7–10), makes more sense if it comes at the end of the present era rather than after a time when Satan has been completely absent, and may be referred to in 2 Thessalonians 2:3–8, which speaks of the final rebellion and 'man of lawlessness' being revealed when 'the one who now holds it back' is 'taken out of the way'. Both passages speak of a restricted evil now and a final unrestricted breakout of Satan immediately prior to the second coming of Jesus.

Summing up, an amillennial reading of Revelation 20 would look like this:

- Restraint of Satan for 1,000 years (i.e. a long time) by the cross (thus releasing the Gentiles to come to Christ)   Rev. 20:1–3
- Spiritual resurrection of martyrs as part of Jesus' resurrection   Rev. 20:4–6
- Rule of Christ with the saints from heaven   Rev. 20:4–6
- Release of Satan at end of the 1,000 years   Rev. 20:7
- Satan conspires to raise an army to attack God's people (possibly led by the 'man of lawlessness' of 2 Thess. 2)   Rev. 20:7–9
- Satan's army destroyed by fire at the second advent   Rev. 20:9
- Satan consigned to the lake of fire forever   Rev. 20:10
- Final general resurrection (Christians and others)   Rev. 20:11–13
- Final judgement of all people   Rev. 20:12–15

The amillennial view also has some problems:

- It seems to weaken the language used of Satan's imprisonment in Revelation 20:1–3. The passage not only speaks of Satan being restrained 'to keep him from deceiving the nations' (v. 3) but also says he is thrown into the Abyss, which is locked and sealed over him. In other words, the passage seems to speak of Satan being removed from the scene of earth for the whole period of '1,000 years'. This doesn't look like what we see in the present era.

- Amillennialists have just as much trouble with Satan being imprisoned by an angel, not Jesus, since his binding is instigated by Jesus' work on the cross.
- Premillennialists point out that a spiritual resurrection in Revelation 20:4–5 seems to fly in the face of the Greek, which uses the same wording of both those who 'came to life' in the first resurrection and those who only came to life after the 1,000 years.
- The second coming of Jesus seems to fit the language of Revelation 19:11–16 (which clearly describes Jesus) better than Revelation 20:9, which says 'fire came down from heaven' but does not mention Jesus. However, the idea of recapitulation may save the amillennialist here: possibly both passages refer to the second coming, but Revelation 20 goes back to the start of the Christian era to re-tell the story from a new perspective.
- However, amillennialists need us to believe that Jesus is ruling and Satan is bound and unable to deceive the nations *at the same time as* Satan is being worshipped and conquering the saints and deceiving 'the inhabitants of the earth' (all those not written in the book of life) through his proxies, the two beasts (Rev. 13). This situation is the result of Satan losing his position in heaven (Rev. 12:7–9) and being 'hurled to the earth' (v. 9) rather than being imprisoned in the Abyss (20:3). There seems to be too great a strain on the language here. Perhaps neither picture really fits with the current situation faced by most believers.
- It is arguable that Revelation makes more sense as a more or less chronological story. While elements of recapitulation seem to be present, there seems to be a coherent plot which comes to a climax in Revelation 19 and then leads us into a new situation in Revelation 20 and following.

3. Postmillennialism

Postmillennialism is the third historical option for reading Revelation 20. Postmillennialists see the 1,000 years as still future (like premillennialists) but prior to the second coming (like amillennialists). Generally they see this as a promise of a period within the Christian era of great victory for the church in the power of the Holy Spirit: huge numbers of people come into the kingdom of God through the preaching of the gospel, the church increases in influence in all aspects of society and Satan is powerless to stop it. However, at the end, Satan is able to make a comeback and establish the 'man of lawlessness' for a short period before the second coming of Christ.

Postmillennialism was very strong among the Puritans and their successors in the seventeenth and eighteenth centuries in Britain and the USA especially, particularly during the great revivals of those times (Jonathan Edwards[214] was a leading exponent). But it lost credibility during the nineteenth and twentieth centuries for two reasons:

- It became too closely allied in thought with liberalism and the social gospel, which over-confidently expected to Christianize the world through social ministries.
- Its optimistic view of the future seemed out of touch with reality in the light of the great wars, persecutions and other disasters of the twentieth century particularly.

Hal Lindsey tried to pronounce its obituary in *The Late Great Planet Earth*. More recently, there has been a modest revival of postmillennialism in two circles: Reformed Christianity (in particular those associated with Reconstructionism) and Pentecostalism. However, it is still a minority in both of those movements.

Reconstructionists believe that the church is mandated to rebuild a Christian culture in the world at large, not only by evangelism but also by political and social means, such as protesting against abortion. Their vision embraces a Christian society resembling the post-Constantinian Roman world (without its worse features) and basing its laws on the Old Testament civil order. This is not the form of postmillennialism under consideration here.

Let's see how a postmillennialist would read Revelation 20:

- Defeat of the beast by Christ and his church   Rev. 19:11–23
- Restraint of Satan for 1,000 years (i.e. a long
  period of time)   Rev. 20:1–3
  (thus releasing the Gentiles to come to Christ in unprecedented numbers through the work of the Holy Spirit)

- Spiritual resurrection of martyrs in the power of
  Jesus' resurrection   Rev. 20:4–6
- Rule of Christ with the saints from heaven   Rev. 20:4–6
  (in the power of the outpoured Spirit, as in Acts 2:33)
- Release of Satan at the end of the 1,000 years   Rev. 20:7
- Satan conspires to raise an army to attack God's
  people (possibly led by the 'man of lawlessness' of
  2 Thess. 2)   Rev. 20:7–9
- Satan's army destroyed by fire at the second
  advent   Rev. 20:9
- Satan consigned to the lake of fire forever   Rev. 20:10
- Final general resurrection (Christians and
  others)   Rev. 20:11–13
- Final judgement of all people   Rev. 20:12–15

This reading has some attractions. Like amillennialism, it sees the ministry of Christ and his church as one and this allows us to read Revelation 19 as a powerful victory of Christ and his church (see Rev. 19:14) over the forces of the evil one rather than Christ alone in his second coming. Also like amillennialism, this reading allows the resurrection and last judgement to be read as one event rather than two stages separated by 1,000 years, a major weakness of premillennialism.

It has some advantages over amillennialism, however. It allows us to read Revelation more naturally as a chronological narrative. Thus the rule of the beasts is *followed* by the triumph of the church rather than them being two aspects of the same situation. Also the binding of Satan by an angel makes more sense (at least to me) if it follows a joint victory of Christ and the church, parallel to Revelation 12:7–11 where Satan loses his place in heaven in an angelic battle released by both 'the blood of the Lamb' and the witness of the saints.

Some other passages also support or are compatible with post-millennialism, such as Revelation 7:9 and John 12:32. Revelation 7:9 speaks of an *innumerable* international company of saved people. This is much more optimistic than most forms of amillennialism or premillennialism. Interestingly, La Haye interprets this passage as predicting an incredibly large harvest during the post-rapture tribulation period, after the removal of the church!

This suggests that God's cause will do much better without us Christians, which may sometimes seem true, but isn't particularly compatible with other passages in the New Testament. It makes more sense to take this passage as promising a huge harvest in the future, since this level of success hasn't been seen before, but using the normal means of this era, largely evangelism.

John 12:32 speaks of Jesus being 'lifted up from the earth' (on the cross, v. 33) and thus drawing 'all men' to himself. This probably does not mean that every person will be saved (universalism) but it is also a very optimistic prediction of the future success of the gospel.[215]

This reading allows us to read Revelation in terms of the triumph of the martyrs using the spiritual or Idealist reading strategy I advocated above. This leads us to the major difficulty with postmillennialism (aside from the problems it shares with amillennialism): it seems *over*-optimistic. Earlier, we noted how the early church used the strategy of witness and prayer drawn from Revelation to conquer Rome. But we then had to face the fact that this was not such a good victory after all: it led to the church becoming corrupted by its position of power and privilege. On a smaller scale, the hopes of the English Puritans for a godly commonwealth were disappointed once they and their allies actually came to power in the seventeenth century. Similarly, the early theocracies established in America soon declined, in spite of great revivals. And the twentieth century shows us that optimism about humanity is very misplaced.

So the only form of postmillennialism that might be justified would be one that is clearly based on an Idealist reading of Revelation. In other words, the promise of the 1,000 years is a real promise and hope set before the church at all times, to stir us to prayer, witness and even social action in the power of the Holy Spirit. But the promise is not a guaranteed prediction. Even when it seems to triumph, the church is in danger of corruption and decline, because Christians are still prone to sin and the devil keeps making comebacks! Moreover, this vision can never be attained by human organization or effort, but only by the power of the Holy Spirit.

Will the millennium ever come? Maybe it depends on Christians who are willing to be overcomers at the cost of their own lives (Rev. 12:11).

Appendix 1

THE PREDICTIVE VALUE OF REVELATION

Prediction	Made by	When	Passage	Fulfilled?
Decline and breakup of the Roman Empire	Lactantius	c.300	17	5th Cent.
Revived Roman confederacy	Hal Lindsey[216]	1970	17:9–13	European Union? (but over 10 nations now)
World dictator	Hal Lindsey	1970	13	??
144,000 Jewish evangelists	Hal Lindsey	1970	7:1–9; 14:1–5	??
Unified world religion	Hal Lindsey	1970	17	??
Imminent monastic renewal	Joachim of Fiore	12th Cent.	8:1	??
Raise of a saintly pope	Joachim of Fiore	12th Cent.	7:2	??

Prediction	Made by	When	Passage	Fulfilled?
Fatal blow to papal power	Various Protestants	17th and 18th Cent.	13:5	1798 Napoleon's victory
Final overthrow of papacy In 1836 In 1866	J. Wesley Thruston	18th Cent. 19th Cent.	17–19	End of papal states in 1870
Fall of Saracens in 1300	Olivi	13th Cent.	13:18	
Fall of Ottoman Empire (Turks)	H. Guinness	1886	16:12	1918
Decline of Islam	H. Guinness	1886	16:12	Early 20th Cent. but res- urgent now
ID markings on forehead	B. Smith J. Beacham	1980s 1993	13:16	??
Overthrow of Parliament in 1650	George Foster	1649	13:17	??
Apperance of Christ in 1688	John Napier	1617	11:15	Glorious Revolution in 1688?
Armageddon in 1914	Jehovah's Witnesses		16	World War I
Chinese-led invasion of Israel	Hal Lindsay	1970	9:16; 9:16; 16:12	??

Prediction	Made by	When	Passage	Fulfilled?
Asian invation of the West	Robert Gromacki	1970	16:12	??
All cities destroyed	Hal Lindsay	1970	16:9	??
Last judgement about 1326	Alexander Minorita	d. 1271	20?	??
Cashless society	J.Beacham	1993	13:16–18	??
UK to leave the EU	T. Foster	1984	16:12	??
Russian Comm-munists to take over Western Europe	T. Foster	1984	16:12	Fall of Soviet bloc in 1990
Nuclear war	Hal Lindsey	1970s	8, 9, 16	??

Appendix 2

THE PREDICTIVE VALUE OF DANIEL

Prediction	Made by	When	Passage	Fulfilled?
Second Coming in 1843/44	William Miller	c. 1830	8:14	Passage of Christ to the Holy of Holies (according to SDAS)
Seven year peace treaty with Israel brokered by the Antichrist	B. Smith Hal Lindsey	1980s 1970	9:27	Several agreements, none lasting, in 1980s and 90s
Restored Jewish temple and sacrifices	Wilbur Smith Hal Lindsay	1949 1970	9:27	??
Egyptian invasion of Israel[217]	Hal Lindsey	1970	11	1973 Yom Kippur war?
Ten-nation European confederacy	Arno Gaebelin	1914	2, 7	European Union

Prediction	Made by	When	Passage	Fulfilled?
The Antichrist ruling 10 nations after banishing 3	J. Beacham	1993	7:19–25	??
End of the Jews' tribulation in 1944	Isaac Newton	17th Cent.	??	1945 perhaps?

Appendix 3

FURTHER READING

If you have been stimulated by this book to read more about *Revelation*, here are some books that will help you. I do not necessarily endorse everything these authors say, but they are valuable resources for the student.

The Use and Misuse of Revelation: Historical Studies of How Revelation Has Been Used and Is Being Interpreted Now

Judith Kovacs and Christopher Rowland, *Revelation* (Blackwell Bible Commentaries; Malden/Oxford: Blackwell Publishing, 2004).
A commentary based on historical uses of Revelation over the centuries, organized under the chapters of Revelation. A major source for my early chapters.

Arthur W. Wainwright, *Mysterious Apocalypse: Interpreting the Book of Revelation* (Nashville: Abingdon Press, 1993).
Tells the story of how the Christians have interpreted Revelation chronologically through church history.

C. Marvin Pate, ed., *Four Views on the Book of Revelation* (Grand Rapids: Zondervan, 1998).
Four scholars present a Preterist view, an Idealist view, a progressive dispensationalist and a classical dispensationalist view of Revelation. Useful but omits some perspectives.

Steve Gregg, ed., *Revelation: Four Views, a Parallel Commentary* (Nashville: Thomas Nelson, 1997).
This book has a great introduction to Revelation and the four views it presents. It then provides in parallel columns a full commentary

from these 4 perspectives: Historicist, Preterist, Futurist and Spiritual (Idealist). The best comparative presentation I have seen.

Introductions to Revelation

Richard Bauckham, *The Theology of the Book of Revelation* (Cambridge: Cambridge University Press, 1993).
Excellent survey of the literary features and teaching of Revelation.
Gilbert Desrosiers, *An Introduction to Revelation* (London: Continuum, 2000).
The best overall introduction to Revelation, its literary features, common interpretations, current issues, etc.
Wes Howard-Brook and Anthony Gwyther, *Unveiling Empire: Reading Revelation Then and Now.* (Maryknoll: Orbis Books, 2003).
Provocative, at times a bit one-sided, but contains a wealth of information about the historical background to Revelation as well as commenting on recent approaches to the text.

Commentaries

Robert W. Wall, *Revelation* New International Biblical Commentary (Peabody: Hendrickson, 1991).
The best shorter commentary, combining good scholarship with readable language.
G.K. Beale, *The Book of Revelation* (New International Greek Testament Commentary; Grand Rapids: Eerdmans, 1999).
The best longer commentary, especially good for relating Revelation *to its Old Testament background.*
Ben Witherington, *Revelation* (New Cambridge Bible Commentary; Cambridge: Cambridge University Press, 2003).
A good mid-range commentary which engages some more recent reading strategies, what he calls a 'socio-rhetorical' approach. Good suggestions for relating Revelation to our lives today in a responsible way.

Other Relevant Books

Stanley J. Grenz, *The Millennial Maze* (Downers Grove: InterVarsity Press, 1992).
A readable, organized, balanced and intelligent discussion of the millennium and the different evangelical views about it, with historical background.

David Chilton, *Days of Vengeance* (Tyler: Dominion Press, 1987).
Set out as a commentary, but not really what I would look for in a commentary, since it is somewhat one-sided, but it is very provocative and stimulating. This author has also written a shorter book on the great tribulation.

Hank Hanegraaff, *The Apocalypse Code* (Nashville: Thomas Nelson, 2007).
Somewhat strident attack on the dispensationalists from a Preterist standpoint.

Kenneth L. Gentry, Jr, *He Shall Have Dominion* (Tyler, TX: Institute for Christian Economics, 1997).
A powerful argument for postmillennialism, albeit with a Reconstructionist flavour, and for a Preterist view of Revelation.

Endnotes

Chapter 1 – Strange Revelations

[1] As quoted in Jacques Chevalier, *A Postmodern Revelation: Signs of Astrology and the Apocalypse* (Toronto: University of Toronto Press, 1997), 368.

[2] Bernard McGinn, as quoted in Paul Boyer, *When Time Shall Be No More* (Cambridge, MA: Belknap Press, 1992), 43; emphasis added.

[3] Dwight Wilson, *Armageddon Now!* (Tyler, TX: Institute for Christian Economics, 1991), xxvii.

[4] Located in modern-day Turkey.

[5] Cf. Boyer, *When Time Shall Be No More*, 46ff.

[6] Judith Kovacs and Christopher Rowland, *Revelation* (Oxford: Blackwell Publishing, 2004), 257.

[7] More on this later.

[8] Kovacs and Rowland, *Revelation*, 141ff.

[9] Boyer, *When Time Shall Be No More*, 51–53.

[10] The first one was Charlemagne (742–814), crowned Holy Roman Empire by Pope Leo III in 800.

[11] Kovacs and Rowland, *Revelation*, 158.

[12] Kovacs and Rowland, *Revelation*, 118ff.

[13] Kovacs and Rowland, *Revelation*, 137ff.

Chapter 2 – How to Misuse Revelation

[14] John F. Walvoord and John E. Walvoord, *Armageddon, Oil and the Middle East Crisis* (Grand Rapids: Zondervan, 1976), 200–204.

[15] Interesting that a New Zealander should find this so significant.

[16] Barry Smith, *Better than Nostradamus or the Secretive World Takeover* (Marlborough, NZ: International Support Ministries, 1996), 67 (emphasis added). In a similar book, Don Stanton talks of the rise of the Antichrist and states, 'I myself am convinced that this will take place before the end of this century. It could even happen within the next seven years.' This was written in 1977! (Don E. Stanton, *Mystery 666*; Secunderabad [Maranatha Revival Crusade, 1977:7]).

[17] Barry R. Smith, *Warning* (Smith Family Evangelism, 1980), *Second Warning* (Smith Family Evangelism, 1985) and others.

[18] E.g. Smith, *Warning*, 75–101.

[19] Smith, *Warning*, 10–21.

[20] Smith, *Warning*, 22–44. Compare Walvoord and Walvoord, *Armageddon*, 113–118, 205. Similar predictions are rife in Dispensationalist books, making every so-called peace accord between Israel and the Arabs highly suggestive: is this the start of the seven-year countdown? As I write, US Secretary of State Condoleeza Rice is trying to revive peace negotiations involving Israel, Egypt and Saudi Arabia. So will George Bush, Jr finally turn out to be the Antichrist? However, as these predictions are largely based on Daniel, I am not discussing them in detail in this book.

[21] Smith, *Warning*, 45–50.

[22] Smith, *Warning*, 30, 31, 35.

[23] Compare to Walvoord and Walvoord, *Armageddon*, 142.

[24] Smith, *Warning*, 64–73.

[25] Smith, *Warning*, 37–43, 100 ff.; Stanton, *Mystery 666*, 50ff.

[26] Wilson, *Armageddon Now!*, 213.

[27] Jeff Beacham, *Apocalypse How?* (Self-published, 1993), 77ff.

[28] Beacham, *Apocalypse How?*, 92.

[39] E.g. H. Grattan Guinness, *The Approaching End of the Age* (London: Hodder & Stoughton, 1886), 379ff., 473ff.

[30] Wilson, *Armageddon Now!*, 32, 99.

[31] Futurists believe that Revelation is mainly about the dying days of the current age, the last few years leading up to the second coming.

[32] E.g. Lindsey, *Late Great Planet Earth*, 55 ff. Cf. Boyer, *When Time Shall Be No More*, 196ff.; LaHaye, *Revelation Unveiled* (Grand Rapids: Zondervan, 1999); Walvoord and Walvoord, *Armageddon*, 72, 95.

[33] Wilson, *Armageddon Now!*, xli–xlii. These stories often turn out to be 'urban myths' when investigated closely (p. 200); similar reports were around in the mid-nineteenth century (p. 26) and the 1950s

(p. 142). However, there is a 'Jerusalem Temple Foundation', which explores ways the temple could be rebuilt (Ibid., xlii), so at least some people have serious intentions here (compare Grant R. Jeffrey, *The Signature of God* [Toronto: Frontier Research Publications, 2002], 201ff.).

³⁴ Wilson, *Armageddon Now!*, 98.

³⁵ Significantly, Paul writes about 'the man of lawlessness' who 'sets himself up in God's temple, proclaiming himself to be God' (2 Thess. 2:3–4).

³⁶ E.g. Beacham, *Apocalypse How?*, 64ff.

³⁷ Cf. Boyer, *When Time Shall Be No More*, 208–216.

³⁸ www.worldslastchance.com/full_article.php (accessed 19/04/2007).

³⁹ This is not an official Seventh-day Adventist site, and actually criticizes Adventists for going soft on Roman Catholicism, but reflects many traditional Adventist teachings. See also Roger Foster, *The Book of Revelation Unveiled* (United Church of God, 2001), 21, 27.

⁴⁰ Cf. Wilson, *Armageddon Now!*, for a lengthy description of premillennialist predictions about Russia and Israel.

⁴¹ E.g. Thomas Foster, *Amazing Book of Revelation Explained!* (Adelaide: Crusade Centre, 1983), 90–116; based on Rev. 16–18. Foster then predicts the downfall of Russia at the hands of the USA and its allies in an air war (Ibid., 94–123; based on Rev. 16:16–18; 19:11–20).

⁴² Wilson, *Armageddon Now!*, 185ff.

⁴³ Wilson, *Armageddon Now!*, 17.

⁴⁴ Wilson, *Armageddon Now!*, 26.

⁴⁵ Beacham, *Apocalypse How?*, 60ff.; see also Jeffrey, *Signature of God*, 216 ff.; Boyer, *When Time Shall Be No More*, 109, 167 ff. describes earlier versions of the 'yellow peril' based on Rev. 16:12.

⁴⁶ Beacham, *Apocalypse How?*, 96.

⁴⁷ Tim LaHaye, *Revelation Unveiled* .

⁴⁸ Cf. LaHaye's comments on growing Chinese might (*Revelation Unveiled*, 256), 10.

⁴⁹ Cf. Boyer, *When Time Shall Be No More*, 281–88. This move is usually seen as part of a conspiracy launched originally by the Illuminati in the eighteenth century and advanced by such diverse groups as the Freemasons, Communists and international bankers (cf. Stanton, *Mystery*, 666).

⁵⁰ These cards are now being withdrawn (2007).

⁵¹ Cf. Boyer, *When Time Shall Be No More*, 331–34.

[52] Smith, *Better than Nostradamus*, 203 (emphasis original).

[53] Catholic brothers following St Francis of Assisi. They lived in poverty as they traveled about doing good.

[54] Kovacs and Rowland, *Revelation*, 19, 55, 85, 100ff.

[55] Often called 'Bloody Queen Mary' because of the number of Protestants burned at the stake under her rule.

[56] Kovacs and Rowland, *Revelation*, 89.

[57] Kovacs and Rowland, *Revelation*, 143.

[58] Kovacs and Rowland, *Revelation*, 169.

[59] Kovacs and Rowland, *Revelation*, 158, 186.

[60] Kovacs and Rowland, *Revelation*, 130ff. King James II, himself a Catholic, was widely suspected of plotting to return England to Catholicism. He was forced to flee in 1688 and replaced by his daughter Mary and her Dutch Protestant husband William III.

[61] Ernest R. Sandeen, *The Roots of Fundamentalism* (Chicago: University of Chicago Press, 1970), 6ff., as quoted in Wilson, *Armageddon Now!*, 19 (emphasis added).

[62] *Seventh-day Adventists Believe . . .* (Washington DC: Ministerial Association, General Conference of Seventh-day Adventists, 1988), 339ff.

[63] *Seventh-day Adventists Believe . . .*, 338–45.

[64] Kovacs and Rowland, *Revelation*, 192ff.

[65] www.watchtower.org (accessed 29/09/07)

[66] The nuclear power plant at Chernobyl in the Ukraine blew up in 1986, causing intense radiation in the area and a cloud of radioactive pollution to blow across northern Europe. This was part of the train of events that led to the downfall of the USSR.

[67] Kovacs and Rowland, *Revelation*, 175; Boyer, *When Time Shall Be No More*, 118 ff.

[68] Boyer, *When Time Shall Be No More*, 127ff., referring to Lindsey's *There's a New World Coming*.

[69] LaHaye, *Revelation Unveiled*, 188; Jeffrey, *Signature of God*, 211.

[70] www.watchtower.org (accessed 29/09/07)

[71] *Seventh-day Adventists Believe . . .*, 154, 160–168.

[72] Kovacs and Rowland, *Revelation*, 48. Stigmata are marks of apparent crucifixion that have been known to appear mysteriously on the hands of some Catholic mystics, even in the present day.

[73] Kovacs and Rowland, *Revelation*, 114.

[74] Kovacs and Rowland, *Revelation*, 128.

[75] E.g. Foster, *Amazing Book,* 34ff., 63–66, 76–83.

[76] Boyer, *When Time Shall Be No More,* 68–77, 84ff., 225–253. Boyer points out a famous contrast with Jesuit Daniel Berrigan's use of Revelation to attack the militarism of the USA (p. 260ff.).

[77] Boyer, *When Time Shall Be No More,* 225.

[78] Cf. Wilson, *Armageddon Now!* Grant Jeffrey does some interesting things with Bible numbers and prophecies to show that the Old Testament specifically predicted the exact date of the birth of the modern state of Israel (Jeffrey, *Signature of God,* 171–76).

[79] E.g. Walvoord and Walvoord, *Armageddon,* 59–100.

[80] LaHaye, *Revelation Unveiled,* 211.

[81] LaHaye, *Revelation Unveiled,* 211, 222, 228, 271ff.

[82] LaHaye, *Revelation Unveiled,* 268–75.

[83] The move to deify Roman emperors and construct temples in their honour. This was especially strong in the province of Asia, to which Revelation was sent.

[84] Kovacs and Rowland, *Revelation,* 178, 184ff. This idea was not invented by Protestants, however, but arose in the late Middle Ages among radical Franciscans and others (p. 178).

[85] Cf. Boyer, *When Time Shall Be No More,* 273ff.

[86] Cf. Peter Ackroyd, *Isaac Newton* (London: Chatto and Windus, 2006), 53–56. In Newton's case, his anti-Catholic views led him to a form of Arianism, rejecting the doctrine of the Trinity, and similar to aspects of Jehovahs Witnesses' beliefs. The full manuscripts of Newton's voluminous writings on biblical prophecy, especially Daniel and Revelation, may be found at http://www.newtonproject.sussex.ac.uk.

[87] Dave Hunt, *A Woman Rides the Beast* (Eugene: Harvest House, 1994).

[88] Kovacs and Rowland, *Revelation,* 7, 188ff.

[89] Kovacs and Rowland, *Revelation,* 178.

[90] Kovacs and Rowland, *Revelation,* 183ff.

[91] Boyer, *When Time Shall Be No More,* 84ff.

[92] Kovacs and Rowland, *Revelation,* 187; Boyer, *When Time Shall Be No More,* 262, 278.

[93] Cf. Beacham, *Apocalypse How?,* 86.

[94] Walvoord and Walvoord, *Armageddon,* 109.

[95] Walvoord and Walvoord, *Armageddon,* 103–109. The World Council of Churches may be justly criticized on many points, but the question is whether it is referred to in Revelation.

[96] Cf. Boyer, *When Time Shall Be No More,* 330; Jeffrey, *Signature of God,* 204 ff.

[97] LaHaye, *Revelation Unveiled*, 279.

[98] *Seventh-day Adventists Believe . . .*, 155ff.

[99] Kovacs and Rowland, *Revelation*, 157. Laud was appointed by King Charles I and was an inveterate enemy of the Puritans.

[100] Boyer, *When Time Shall Be No More*, 72.

[101] Kovacs and Rowland, *Revelation*, 157ff.; Boyer, *When Time Shall Be No More*, 108.

[102] Boyer, *When Time Shall Be No More*, 108.

[103] Kovacs and Rowland, *Revelation*, 156ff.

[104] Kovacs and Rowland, *Revelation*, 152.

[105] Cf. Boyer, *When Time Shall Be No More*, 276ff.

[106] Kovacs and Rowland, *Revelation*, 109.

[107] Kovacs and Rowland, *Revelation*, 114.

[108] Kovacs and Rowland, *Revelation*, 212.

[109] Kovacs and Rowland, *Revelation*, 115.

[110] Lindsey, *Late Great Planet*, 81–87. See comments in Boyer, *When Time Shall Be No More*, 167ff., and also Wilson, *Armageddon Now!*, 118ff.

[111] Kovacs and Rowland, *Revelation*, 165. Another seventeenth-century case was the 'Fifth Monarchy Men', a group of radical Puritans who expected the fifth kingdom, after the four empires described in Daniel, to arise soon, with their help (Wilson, *Armageddon Now!*, 17).

[112] Cyrus overthrew the Babylonian empire and allowed the Jews to return to Jerusalem and rebuild the temple (cf. Ezra 1).

[113] Craig R. Koester, *Revelation and the End of All Things* (Grand Rapids: Eerdmans, 2001), 17ff.

[114] Kovacs and Rowland, *Revelation*, 120.

[115] Kovacs and Rowland, *Revelation*, 109.

[116] Kovacs and Rowland, *Revelation*, 198. This is a reference to Rev. 19:11-21.

Chapter 3 – The Left Behind Threat

[117] This is based on the assumption that innocent babies automatically go to heaven if they die. La Haye has thought of everything!

[118] Cf. Boyer, *When Time Shall Be No More*, 106.

[119] Part of the Roman province of Asia, now modern Turkey.

[120] LaHaye, *Revelation Unveiled*, 82.

[121] LaHaye, *Revelation Unveiled*, 172, commenting on Revelation 9.

122 LaHaye, *Revelation Unveiled*, 100.

123 LaHaye, *Revelation Unveiled*, 106.

124 LaHaye, *Revelation Unveiled*, 148.

125 LaHaye, *Revelation Unveiled*, 156–62. In many ways, this move of God resembles the current worldwide expansion of Pentecostal-charismatic Christianity, but I'm not sure if La Haye approves of that.

126 LaHaye, *Revelation Unveiled*, 161.

127 This 'first resurrection' is variously understood by interpreters as referring to the spiritual resurrection of Christian converts (see Eph. 2:4–5; John 5:24), the resurrection of all believers at the second coming (see 1 Thess. 4:4–16; 1 Cor. 15:50–55) or perhaps the resurrection of Jesus himself (see 1 Cor. 15:20–23; Matt. 27:51–53; 28:18–20).

128 Cf. LaHaye, *Revelation Unveiled*, 143.

129 See LaHaye, *Revelation Unveiled*, 182ff.

130 See NIV margin.

131 Cf. 1 John 2:18–22; 4:3.

132 Interestingly, a Catholic commentator, Robert Bellarmine (d.1621), believed that 'the Antichrist is an individual Jew, reigning in Jerusalem for three and a half years' (Kovacs and Rowland, *Revelation*, 212).

Chapter 4 – Bad Interpretations

133 Newton wrote extensively on Revelation but his views were never mainstream. Cf. Ackroyd, *Isaac Newton*, 52–56, 146–151.

134 This is the view that Revelation mainly speaks about its own day or the near future.

135 Christian Revival Crusade, founded by the late Leo Harris, and still strong in southern Australia. A more controversial offshoot was the Revival Centres, who still hold this view strongly.

136 Charles Taylor, *Revelation as World History* (Gosford: Good Book Company, 1994), 28.

137 Taylor, *World History*, 57.

138 Old Testament support for this principle is found in Num. 14:34; Ezek. 4:5, 6; and Dan. 12:11–12.

139 How that happened is too complex to tell here, but Adventists take their name from this view. While many modern Adventists sit lightly with their traditional doctrines, more 'fundamentalist' groups are still trumpeting loudly that the pope is (or is soon to become) the

Antichrist, and that Sunday observance is (or is soon to become) the mark of the beast. For a good description of the rise of Millerism, see Stephen D. O'Leary, *Arguing the Apocalypse* (Oxford: Oxford University Press, 1994), 93–133.

[140] K. Bickel, *Prophetic Time Periods in History and the Final Hour*; Adelaide: BI-CK-EL Publishing, 1995 (originally 1992). The author's name appears to be a pseudonym, abbreviating 'Bene yisrael kedoshim leadonai'.

[141] Bickel, *Time Periods*, iv.

[142] Bickel, *Time Periods*, 59, 120ff.

[143] Bickel, *Time Periods*, 123ff.

[144] Bickel, *Time Periods*, 98.

[145] Bickel, *Time Periods*, 121ff. Wilson summarizes a similar calculative effort by W.E. Blackstone (reported in 1916) which led to the significant dates being 1916, 1927 and 1935 (Wilson, *Armageddon Now!*, 40 ff.). Christabel Pankhurst saw 1925 as likely to see the confederation of nations leading to the Antichrist (p. 63).

[146] Both Rev. 19 and 2 Thess. 2 (which Historicists use extensively) depict the Antichrist being overthrown by the parousia (second coming), so Taylor must talk of its power being 'reduced' at the end of the tribulation while it awaits the parousia (*World History*, 83). Similarly, Guinness writes of a two-stage doom 'gradual consumption, followed by sudden and final destruction' (*Approaching the End*, 218). He regards the former as in progress in his day (1886) in the loss of power by the popes, 'exactly' 1260 years since its rise in the early seventh century! (p. 465ff.). Therefore 'Its days are numbered. Its end is near' (p. 223).

[147] *Explanatory Notes*, 1026.

[148] Taylor, *World History*, 88.

[149] Cf. LaHaye, *Revelation Unveiled*, 140.

[150] Thus chapters 2–3 would function for these Futurists as the whole book does for Historicists.

[151] LaHaye, *Revelation Unveiled*, 36.

[152] Preterists see Revelation as describing events in John's day or soon after.

[153] Joel Richardson, *AntiChrist: Islam's Awaited Messiah* (Enumclaw: Pleasant Word, 2006).

[154] Cf. Steve Gregg, ed., *Revelation: Four Views* (Nashville: Thomas Nelson, 1997), 32ff.; LaHaye, *Revelation Unveiled*, 110.

155 John F. Walvoord, *The Revelation of Jesus Christ* (Chicago: Moody Press, 1966), 8. See also Thomas, *Revelation 1–7*, 36; LaHaye, *Revelation Unveiled*, 17.

156 For instance, Walvoord contends, 'The concept that the book of Revelation beginning with 4:1 is future . . . is a broad conclusion growing out of the lack of correspondence of these prophecies to anything that has been fulfilled', *The Revelation*, 101, see also 102; and G. E. Ladd, *A Commentary on the Revelation of John* (Grand Rapids: Eerdmans, 1972), 181.

157 Merrill C. Tenney, *Interpreting Revelation* (Grand Rapids: Eerdmans, 1957), 75.

158 Tenney, *Revelation*.

159 Cf. G.K. Beale, *Book of Revelation* (New International Greek Testament commentary; Grand Rapids: Eerdmans, 1999), 58–64, about John's symbolic use of numbers.

160 LaHaye, *Revelation Unveiled*, 17, see also 251.

161 LaHaye, *Revelation Unveiled*, 219.

162 LaHaye, *Revelation Unveiled*, 222.

163 See comments by Gary North in the 'Publisher's Preface' to Wilson, *Armageddon Now!*, x–xv.

164 E.g. LaHaye, *Revelation Unveiled*, 140.

165 I am not denying the possibility of long-range predictive prophecy. This clearly happens in Scripture. But it is nearly always related to the situation of the human author's day and is never the dominant feature of any prophetic book.

166 I expect Tony Blair (former UK Prime Minister) may emerge as a candidate now that he has taken on the unenviable role of Middle East peacemaker, especially now that he has become a Roman Catholic.

167 For another argument against literalism as the hermeneutical approach to Revelation, based particularly on Rev. 1:1, see Beale, *Book of Revelation*, 50–55.

168 Ladd, *Revelation*, 234.

169 Ladd, *Revelation*, 221ff.

170 Ladd, *Revelation*, 222. Robert Thomas offers a different possibility: Babylon is literally a future Babylon (on the Euphrates). But to maintain this he has to 'spiritualize' the seven hills of Rev. 17:9 – 'the seven hills refer to the scope and nature of the beast's power' (Thomas, 'A Classical Dispensationalist View', 202ff.).

Chapter 5 – The Value of Revelation

[171] Koester, *End of All Things*, 32.

[172] Of course, in these days of suicide bombers the concept of martyr-dom is very suspect. Christian martyrs throughout history have never been violent themselves (except perhaps in their language sometimes) and most Christian theologians reserve the term 'martyr' for those who are killed or suffer violence because of their witness or service to Jesus. Christians have sometimes committed violence (regrettably) but such are not regarded as martyrs.

[173] Cf. Kovacs and Rowland, *Revelation*, 216.

[174] Cf. Kovacs and Rowland, *Revelation*, 9–10, 23–24, 96, 216.

[175] Cf. Kovacs and Rowland, *Revelation*, 116, 179, 191, 234.

[176] Cf. Kovacs and Rowland, Revelation, 36–37, 95.

[177] For the full text, see Kovacs and Rowland, *Revelation*, 90–91.

[178] Koester, *End of All Things*, 33–38.

[179] Some of these verses may not refer to the final return of Christ, but some certainly do.

[180] Some of these verses may refer to earlier stages of God's judgement, such as the destruction of Jerusalem in AD 70.

[181] Ancient Jewish documents resembling Revelation in some areas have been called 'apocalypses' (the name being taken from Rev. 1:1). These books often have a very complex doctrine of angels, naming them in greater precision and giving them greater roles than the Bible. See below, n. 183.

[182] One commentator called Revelation 'a vision of a just world'.

Chapter 6 – Responsible Interpretations

[183] Apocalypses were books of prophecy resembling Revelation in certain ways (e.g. weird symbolic visions, angelic interpreters, focus on coming judgement). Jewish authors produced many such texts around the time of Jesus; the most famous was 1 Enoch, supposedly containing prophecies by Enoch, who lived before the Flood, but most likely written in the first century BC. There were also early Christian apocalypses; the most famous was the Shepherd of Hermas. See David E. Aune, *Revelation 1–5* (Dallas: Word Books, 1997), lxx–xc.

[184] Some good sources on this include Wes Howard-Brook and Anthony Gwyther, *Unveiling Empire: Reading Revelation Then and Now* (Maryknoll: Orbis Books, 2003) and, more briefly, Ben Witherington, *Revelation* (Cambridge: Cambridge University Press, 2003), 5–10, 22–27. See also note 190 below.

[185] The occasion of writing refers to the historical situation of the author, the experiences or news that prompted him/her to write.

[186] Funnily enough, the letters named 1, 2 and 3 John are anonymous, and the Gospel of John only hints at its author, while Revelation actually claims to be written by John.

[187] For instance, see the creative and at least partly convincing proposals in Kym Smith, *Redating the Revelation and . . .* (Blackwood, SA: Sherwood Publications, 2001) and Gonzalo Rojas-Flores, 'The Book of Revelation and the First Years of Nero's Reign'; *Biblica* 85 (2004): 375–392.

[188] Though this is often now disputed.

[189] *Against Heresies*, 5:30:1, 3 (as quoted in Gregg, ed., *Four Views*, 17).

[190] E.g. Steven J. Friesen, *Imperial Cults and the Apocalypse of John* (Oxford Scholarship Online; Oxford University Press, 2005), which uses particularly archaeological evidence to provide historical background to Revelation; Adela Yarbro Collins, *The Combat Myth in the Book of Revelation* (Missoula: Scholars Press, 1976), which raises important issues concerning the cultural and literary background of Revelation; S.R.F. Price, *Rituals and Power* (Cambridge: Cambridge University Press, 1984), the most comprehensive study of the emperor cult in Asia Minor; Leonard L. Thompson, *The Book of Revelation: Apocalypse and Empire* (Oxford: Oxford University Press, 1990); studies on particular cities in Asia such as Giancarlo Biguzzi, 'Ephesus, Its Artemision, Its Temple to the Flavian Emperors, and Idolatry in Revelation' (*Novum Testamentum* XL, 1998: 276–90) and Craig R. Koester, 'The Message to Laodicea and the Problem of Its Local Context: A Study of the Imagery in Rev. 3.14–22' (*New Testament Studies* 49, 2003: 407–24); and more general texts such as Bruce J. Malina, *The New Testament World* (Louisville: Westminster John Knox Press, 2001).

[191] Cf. Steven J. Scherrer, 'Signs and Wonders in the *Imperial Cult*', *Journal of Biblical Literature* 103/4 (1984): 599–610

[192] E.g. Brian Yhearm, *The Sitz im Leben of Revelation* (PhD thesis, University of Newcastle upon Tyne, 1995), 377; Robert M. Royalty, Jr., *The Streets of Heaven* (Macon, CA: Mercer University Press, 1998), 28.

[193] Cf. Zegwaart, 'Apocalyptic Eschatology', 6.

[194] Nero Caesar fits if translated into Hebrew; Lateinos was one of the possibilities considered in early Christian commentary.

[195] Some recent studies include Steve Moyise, *The Old Testament in the Book of Revelation* (Sheffield: Sheffield Academic Press, 1995); G.K. Beale, *John's Use of the Old Testament in Revelation* (Sheffield: Sheffield Academic Press, 1998); Richard Bauckham, *The Climax of Prophecy* (Edinburgh: T&T Clark, 1993). Many of the OT references are set out in column forms in Conner, *Interpreting Revelation*, 36–41, 45–49.

[196] Cf. Conner, *Interpreting Revelation*, 42–45.

[197] See William J. Dumbrell, *The End of the Beginning* (Homebush West: Lancer Books, 1985).

[198] As shown by its use of rhetorical strategies (cf. de Smidt, 'Hermeneutical Perspectives', 31ff.). The goal of the text is discussed in the next chapter.

[199] Cf. Bauckham, *The Theology of the Book of Revelation*.

[200] Mathias Rissi, *Time and History* (Richmond: John Knox Press, 1965); Paul S. Minear, 'The Cosmology of the Apocalypse' in William Klassen and Graydon F. Snyder, eds., *Current Issues in New Testament Interpretation* (London: SCM Press, 1962).

Chapter 7 – Why Did John Write Revelation?

[201] The Roman writers who made these sorts of allegations are frequently seen as biased. They had every reason to attack Domitian in order to curry favour with his successors.

[202] Surviving examples of this genre include Longus' *Daphnis and Chloe* (late second century), Xenophon's *Ephesian Romance* (second century), and Chariton's *Chaereas and Callirhoe* (first century, roughly contemporary with Revelation).

[203] E.g. the stories of Jacob and Rachel (Gen. 29:16–30) and Boaz and Ruth (Ruth 2–4).

[204] E.g. the story of Joseph and Aseneth, based on the single reference in Gen. 41:45.

[205] Constantine had a kind of vision before a major battle while he was contending for control of the empire. This vision (and other factors, such as his mother's influence) led him to proclaim freedom and

tolerance for Christians. But he went further, promoting Christianity as a new binding faith for the Roman world and favouring the Christian church and its leaders legally and financially. While this change was no doubt very welcome to the church of that day, unfortunately it led to compromise and the rise of 'nominal Christians'. Gradually the church became embroiled in politics as the Middle Ages dawned.

[206] LaHaye, *Revelation Unveiled*, 52.

[207] Paul may have had a similar idea when he wrote to the Colossian church, 'I am now rejoicing in my sufferings for your sake, and in my flesh I am completing what is lacking in Christ's afflictions for the sake of his body, that is, the church' (Col. 1:24).

[208] Rodney Stark, in his argument about how Christianity grew in the ancient world, spends some time speaking of the part played by large scale epidemics that hit pagans disproportionately hard and gave the Christians the opportunity to demonstrate God's love by caring for the sick at risk to their own lives (see Rodney Stark, *The Rise of Christianity* [Harper SanFrancisco, 1997], chapter 4). When Stark described how one-quarter to one-third of the empire died in the late second century, I could not help being reminded of Rev. 6:8 and 8:11.

Chapter 8 – The Relevance of Revelation Today

[209] Some Futurist books make much of increases in such tragedies in recent days. Some of this comes from a short historical memory, but natural disasters in themselves do not prove the second coming is particularly close.

[210] Capital cities respectively of the northern kingdom of Israel and southern kingdom of Judah formed after the split in Israel after the death of Solomon.

[211] This term comes from set theory, but has been applied to Christian thought when it concentrates on drawing boundaries between true Christians and others, e.g. by asking what doctrines must people believe in order to be 'saved'. Others have proposed a 'centred set' analogy, concentrating more on how close a person is to Jesus. Probably both analogies have their place.

[212] The belief that unbelievers are destroyed completely and thus have no existence after being cast into the lake of fire.

[213] The belief that ultimately all people (perhaps even the devil) will be reconciled to God as a result of suffering punishment in hell. Hence hell will eventually be empty.

Chapter 9 – What About the Millenium?

[214] A leading preacher in the USA during the 'Great Awakening'. Thousands came to Christ through him and he was also an outstanding theologian and philosopher.

[215] Other passages that contain similar optimism include Acts 1:8; 2:17–21; Rom. 11:25–32; Phil. 2:9–11; Col. 1:6; Rev. 5:9–10; 15:4.

Appendix 1 – The Predictive Value of Revelation

[216] Cf. Hal Lindsey, *The Late Great Planet Earth* (Melbourne: S. John Bacon, 1970).

Appendix 2 – The Predicted Value of Daniel

[217] Many similar commentators have predicted a Russian-led invasion of Israel based on Ezekiel 38–39 (e.g. Beacham, *Apocalypse How?*, 67–70).

What Are We Waiting For?

Christian Hope and Contemporary Culture

edited by Stephen Holmes and Russell Rook

What is the contemporary relevance of Christian beliefs about the future? People often feel that a biblical theology of future hope is of little practical value for life in the present. Christians are suspected of waiting for a 'pie in the sky when they die' instead of dealing with the 'steak on their plate while they wait'. But the writers in this book argue that eschatology – the theology of creation's future in God's purposes – is profoundly relevant for contemporary life. This book brings together respected Christian teachers in order to address the pressing question of the relevance of eschatology. It outlines the ideas of the Old and the New Testaments as well as historical Christian teachings on eschatology. Then it creatively explores their implications in an accessible way for a range of current issues: mission, the imagination, music, popular culture, politics, ecology, work, ethics, understanding what it is to be human.

> 'Provocative, accessible stuff that is a vital lifeline to those who have lost hope about Hope.' – **Jeff Lucas**, author, speaker, broadcaster

> 'A comprehensive and compelling overview of a much neglected topic.' – **Mark Stibbe**, speaker and author (anewkindofchristian.com)

Stephen Holmes is a Baptist minister and Lecturer in Theology at the University of St Andrews.

Russell Rook works with Central Government, Local Authorities, local churches and other groups to deliver community regeneration through innovative public services and social enterprise.

978-1-84228-602-0

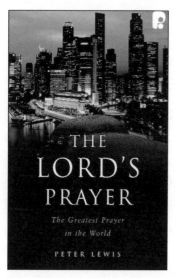

The Lord's Prayer

The Greatest Prayer in the World

Peter Lewis

'Our Father . . .' Quoted, memorised, spoken and sung, the Lord's Prayer is an inspiration to millions. Down the centuries and around the world it has expressed the deepest longings of all true Christians. However, the prayer that Jesus taught his followers reveals something far greater – the character and purposes of God himself. In this sensitive and often moving book, Peter Lewis shows how an intimate relationship with God is a reality that can be experienced today.

> 'When Peter Lewis comes out with a book, the church is always enriched.'
> – **R.T. Kendall**

> 'Peter Lewis is one of the most worshipful pastors I know. His wisdom, humanity and sheer adoration of the greatness of God shine though in this inspirational new edition of *The Lord's Prayer*. It isn't simply an inspiring guide to prayer but also a masterful, tender and powerful entry-level guide to the whole of the Christian life.' – **Julian Hardyman,** Senior Pastor, Eden Baptist Church, Cambridge, England

Peter Lewis leads The Cornerstone Church in Nottingham, England. He has an international speaking ministry and has authored several books.

978-1-84227-601-3

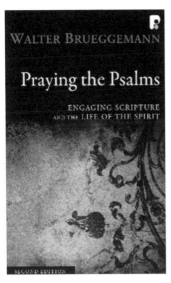

Praying the Psalms

Enaging Scripture and the Life of the Spirit

Walter Brueggemann

Walter Brueggemann pushes his readers to recognize the full gamut of passions reflected in the Psalms: joy and exultation but also disappointment, sorrow, anger, resentment, even the desire for vengeance. We are invited into a daring relationship with the God who calls us to pray with *honesty*. In this spiritual classic readers are guided into a thoughtful and prayerful encounter with God through the Psalms. This new edition includes a thoroughly revised text, new notes, and new bibliography.

> 'Few persons have so lived in and with the Psalms as Walter Brueggemann. Here he takes us into their depths, which are so clearly the depths of our human existence. The piety of the Psalms is strong medicine. Brueggemann bids us take it for the cure of our souls.' – **Patrick D. Miller**, Professor of Old Testament, Princeton Theological Seminary, USA

> 'In *Praying the Psalms*, Brueggemann carefully guides us away from the bland colours of contemporary culture and into the ancient and extreme world of praise and lament. This is essential reading.' – **Ian Stackhouse**, Senior Pastor, Guildford Baptist Church, England

Walter Brueggemann is William Marcellus McPheeters Professor of Old Testament Emeritus at Columbia Theological Seminary, Decatur, Georgia.

978-1-84227-555-9

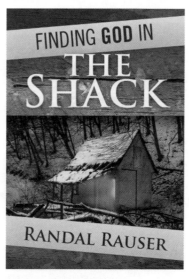

Finding God in
The Shack

Randal Rauser

Aware both of the excitement and uncertainty generated by *The Shack*, theologian Randal Rauser takes the reader on a fascinating journey through the pages of the story. In successive chapters he explores many of the book's complex and controversial issues. Thus he explains why God the Father is revealed as an African American woman, he defends the book's theology of the Trinity against charges of heresy, and he considers its provocative denial of a Trinitarian hierarchy. But at its heart *The Shack* is a response to evil, and so Rauser spends the final three chapters considering the book's explanation for why God allows evil, how the atoning work of Christ offers new hope for a suffering world, and ultimately how this hope extends to all of creation. Through these chapters Rauser offers an honest and illuminating discussion which opens up a new depth to the conversation while providing the reader with new opportunities for finding God in *The Shack*.

'If you have ever had a conversation on *The Shack*, whether with an enthusiast or a critic, you will want to invite this skilled and accessible theologian into the conversation. Before you have read a dozen pages you will know why we need to keep company with theologians like Randel Rauser.' – **Eugene H. Peterson,** Professor Emeritus of Spiritual Theology Regent College, Vancouver, B.C.

'A scholarly specialist on Trinitarian issues engages with the explosive "popular-level" novel – *The Shack*: the outcome is a searching and helpfully revealing theological analysis, and one which is also a generous commendation of Young's contribution on trinity and where "tragedy confronts eternity".' – **Max Turner**, Professor of New Testament Studies, London School of Theology

Randal Rauser is Associate Professor of Historical Theology at Taylor Seminary, Canada and author of *Faith Lacking Understanding* (Paternoster).

978-1-606570-32-6

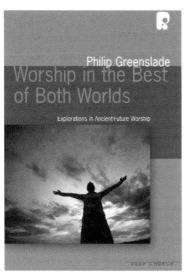

Worship in the Best of Both Worlds

Explorations in Ancient–Future Worship

Philip Greenslade

There are various tensions in Christian worship and, rather than opting for a balanced approach or a one-sided approach, Philip Greenslade recommends that Christians learn to embrace both extremes of each polarity.

- Worship is about glorifying God by enjoying him. So it is about pleasing God and self.
- Worship is world affirming (with a positive view of creation) and world denying (confronting fallen political powers).
- Worship is charismatic and liturgical.
- Worship is a transforming intimacy and an engagement with transcendent majesty.
- Worship is both prophetic praise and realistic lament.
- Worship remembers the past and anticipates the future.
- Worship embraces spontaneous, instinctive cries and a learned language.
- Worship is Trinitarian and Christ-centred.
- It is by worshipping at the extremes that we can experience deeper riches in our knowledge of God.

'Here is a biblical vision of worship at the extremes that is ancient yet ever new. Worship as God-centered, passionate, intimate, world-shaping, explosive, politically subversive, brutally honest, prophetic, Spirit-led and yet rooted in tradition. If this does not inspire you to worship then you may be dead!' – **Robin Parry**, author of Worshipping Trinity

Philip Greenslade has been a full time lecturer and tutor with CWR since 1991 and is the general editor of the Cover to Cover Bible study notes.

978-1-84227-614-3

Debating Darwin

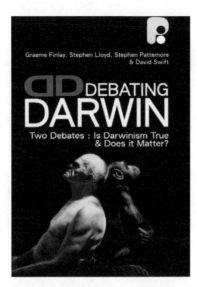

Two Debates: Is Darwinism True and Does it Matter?

Graeme Finlay, Stephen Lloyd, Stephen Pattemore and David Swift

Christians continue to disagree about whether Darwinism should be baptised into our theology or rejected as anti-Christian. This book is aimed at Christians on both sides of the debate and hopes to further discussion by giving space for an open airing of the case both ways. Two distinct questions are under the microscope.

1. Is Darwinism compatible with orthodox Christian faith?
2. Does the scientific evidence support Darwinism?

The book begins with a simple explanation of the neo-Darwinian theory of evolution. Stephen Lloyd then opens the first debate by making a theological and biblical case against Darwinism. He is met in 'battle' by Graeme Finlay and Stephen Patterson who argue that Christian Scripture and theology are compatible with Darwinism. Each set of authors then has a chance to respond to their opponents. In the second debate David Swift argues that whilst the science does support micro-evolution by natural selection it does not support macro-evolution. In fact, he says, the science *undermines* neo-Darwinian claims. 'Not so!' says Graeme Finlay, who argues that the latest work in genetics demonstrates the truth of neo-Darwinism beyond reasonable doubt. Swift and Finlay then interact with each other. This book will not tell readers what to think but it will inform the more intelligent debate.

978-1-932805-619-8